At the age of nineteen, **Kenny McGovern** was diagnosed with what is known as 'Social Anxiety Disorder' and eventually became too ill to carry on working. As the years passed, he became almost housebound as a result of his illness and as such lost touch with many parts of life which although enjoyable are often taken for granted. Simple pleasures such as buying a nice sandwich from a local café or going out for a meal became impossible for him to do.

As a result of this, and because of his love of food and cooking, he eventually took to trying to recreate many of his favourite shop-bought foods at home. 'If I can't go to McDonald's, I'll make my own,' was his philosophy. Over a period of five years or more, he tested and tweaked many, many recipes, his new hobby quickly building into an obsession.

In 2010 Kenny decided to publish some selected recipes in his first book, *The Takeaway Secret: How to Cook Your Favourite Fast-Food at Home*. It became an instant bestseller, following word-of-mouth recommendations on the internet.

With huge support and encouragement from readers, his confidence has grown, along with his food obsession. As a result, Kenny has ventured into the world again, researching and learning about the historic links between street food and local people and the recent upsurge in the modern, exciting and vibrant street food culture. This book is the result.

D1635363

OTHER TITLES

The Takeaway Secret

The Busy Mum's Plan-ahead Cookbook

Eat Well, Spend Less

The Healthy Lifestyle Diet Cookbook

The Everyday Halogen Oven Cookbook

Slow Cook, Fast Food

The Air Fryer Cookbook

Superfood Soups

THE STREET FOOD SECRET

Kenny McGovern

A *How to* Book

ROBINSON

ROBINSON

First published in Great Britain in 2017 by Robinson

5 7 9 10 8 6 4

Copyright © Kenny McGovern, 2017

A CIP catalogue record for this book
is available from the British Library.

ISBN: 978-1-47213-906-1

Typeset in New Caledonia by Hewer Text UK Ltd, Edinburgh
Printed and bound in Great Britain by Clays Ltd, Elcograf S.p.A.

Papers used by Robinson are from well-managed
forests and other responsible sources.

Robinson
An imprint of
Little, Brown Book Group
Carmelite House
50 Victoria Embankment
London EC4Y 0DZ

An Hachette UK Company
www.hachette.co.uk

www.littlebrown.co.uk

With love and thanks to my mum, dad, brother and sister for a lifetime of support and for listening to endless hours of food talk and never looking bored when being asked to look through one hundred food pictures on my phone. Thanks to my niece and nephew for their encouragement and assistance in testing desserts and sweet dishes. Thanks to my fiancée for everything, every day. To John and Audrey for building an amazing kitchen for recipe testing and a conservatory for relaxing. To Adele for eagerly helping test recipes and always helping tidy up afterwards. To Frank for being a friend in food. To Jessica for being the happiest soul I'll ever meet. To Lucy the pussycat who has made herself part of the family. To my family and friends in America for all their help in researching this book. For Granny, and everyone who ever knew and loved her.

CONTENTS

2. RIBS, WINGS & SKEWERS

3. TACOS, WRAPS & SANDWICHES

4. FRYING TONIGHT

5. STIR-FRIES, SOUPS & CURRIES

6. RICE & NOODLES

7. ON THE SIDE

THE STREET FOOD SECRET

8. DESSERTS & DRINKS

CONTENTS

PREFACE

As readers of my first book, *The Takeaway Secret*, will know all too well, my interest in cooking came about as a result of my difficulties with Social Anxiety Disorder. Having become almost completely housebound at one stage, I took to trying to recreate my favourite foods, which had suddenly become out of reach. Being open and honest about the effects the illness was having on my life was, without a doubt, one of the best decisions I've ever made. I was of course delighted that the recipes were proving popular with readers and to this day remain excited when people send me pictures of their creations. The encouragement and feedback I also received from readers in relation to my Social Anxiety, however, was unexpected and very greatly appreciated.

In recent years, with the support of family and friends and with my food obsession still raging, I've managed to expand my horizons hugely and experience a world of food adventures across various countries. Attending street food festivals along the East Coast of the United States sparked a new obsession and one I'm joined in celebrating by many millions of people around the world.

The real beauty of street food is that each dish is tailor-made to provide 100 per cent satisfaction to the customer. With such healthy competition and a fast turnover of people, street vendors need to devise a dish that can be served quickly but always to a high standard in order to ensure the customer remembers them and returns for more. Every mouthful matters and so dishes are created with full-on flavour in mind.

Of course, as home cooks we're ultimately looking for the very same thing when we prepare food at home. Crowd-pleasing dishes made easy, thanks to prior preparation, and finished quickly when our guests (or we ourselves!) are ready to eat. So, with an open and curious mind, I hope you'll enjoy *The Street Food Secret* . . .

Kenny McGovern

INTRODUCTION

The story of street food is the story of people, politics, places and personalities. At its heart, street food is the food of the people. Its heritage and history stand proud and can boast of having kept thousands, if not millions of people alive and nourished where they might otherwise have gone without. Providing inexpensive meals to the poorest people in villages and towns around the world, many of the simplest and humblest of street foods are now enjoyed and celebrated by the wealthiest people in the fanciest restaurants. However, these dishes aren't in need of improving or glamorising, as the classics amongst them have been tried and tested on the city streets for generation after generation.

In contrast to its history and heritage, it's fair to say modern-day street food is undergoing something of a revolution. With the rise of social media, food trucks are building up solid reputations and customer bases, even to the extent of being followed religiously on their travels by customers who just can't get enough of their favourite dishes. Chefs of all backgrounds are creating their own brands and even their own

3

sub-genres of food, bringing together ideas from East and West to create vibrant, modern dishes. It's just one of the many benefits of the multicultural society we live in that we experience and share food ideas amongst each other and there's no better example of togetherness and inclusion than the street-food scene.

For hungry customers, competition amongst vendors results in increased choice and higher standards overall – many chefs focus on just one dish, practising and honing it until it becomes as close to perfection as is possible. The constant evolution of dishes means that the customer is the lucky benefactor and is able to enjoy the best the planet has to offer. As the years go by, more talented chefs will offer their own take on classic dishes and the scene will continue to grow from strength to strength. Street food not only has a long history, it also has a bright future!

Please note

- Large eggs are used in all the recipes.

- All honey used in the recipes is clear.

- Although serving amounts are indicated throughout the book, recipes may be halved or doubled etc. as desired, with good results. Of course, in the case of fried foods or stir-fry dishes, food should be cooked in batches in order to avoid overcrowding in the pan.

  Where ingredients are concerned, please do experiment as and when the situation feels right or, through lack of ingredients, is necessary. Many a good recipe has come about as the result of enforced changes.

- Typically I use sunflower oil for deep-frying. However, lately I've been cooking more with coconut oil due to the apparent health benefits. Here, all the recipes list vegetable oil for deep-frying – the choice is yours!

1

BURGERS & DOGS

A trip to New York City would be incomplete without picking up a hot dog from one of the many street vendors. So fierce is the competition, it's not unheard of for street sellers to pay upwards of $100k for the best pitches in the city! Regulations and red tape in different cities often means vendors travel to locations where they'll be able to go about their business uninterrupted. Sadly, not every city has a positive view on street food trucks and so, when you are fortunate enough to spend time in a place which embraces that culture, it's only polite to indulge in it as often as possible!

Burgers and hot dogs are of course perfect barbecue food and should the weather be suitable, the recipes included in this chapter will provide excellent results if finished on a charcoal grill or the equivalent. The sounds and smells of an outdoor grill are hard to beat and in most cases, where the opportunity exists, it's the preferred option. That said, there are certainly enough exciting flavours and ingredients to make indoor cooking more than worthwhile too.

JUICY LUCY

Serves 1

How to ensure your burger is juicy in the middle? Stuff the patty with delicious melting cheese!

Around 160g beef mince (minimum 20 per cent fat)
Pinch of sea salt and black pepper
½ teaspoon Worcestershire sauce
Pinch of garlic powder
1 processed cheese slice
1 brioche burger bun
1 tablespoon tomato ketchup
2 teaspoons yellow (American) mustard
1 tablespoon finely chopped onion
4 thin gherkin slices
French fries, to serve

- In a bowl, add the beef mince, sea salt, black pepper, Worcestershire sauce and a pinch of garlic powder. Mix well.

- Divide the mixture in half. Using a sheet of greaseproof paper, flatten the mince into two large thin patties. Place the cheese slice in the middle of one of the patties. Add the remaining patty on top, pinching the edges of the two patties together to form a seal. Cover and set aside in the refrigerator for 10 minutes.

- Heat a dry flat frying pan over a medium-high heat. Halve the burger bun and toast face down in the pan for around 30 seconds or until golden. Set aside.

- Place the burger patty onto the hot dry pan and cook for 2–3 minutes. The patty will swell as the burger cooks. Flip the burger and use a fork to pierce a few holes in the top of it. Cook for a further 2 minutes, or until cooked through and the juices run clear.

- Assemble the burger: Spread tomato ketchup and yellow mustard over the bottom burger bun half. Place the cooked Juicy Lucy burger on top. Garnish with chopped onion and gherkin slices. Add the remaining bun half, wrap the burger in foil or baking paper and place in the oven at the lowest available setting for 2–3 minutes to combine flavours and heat through. Serve with French fries.

CALIFORNIA GREENING

Serves 1

Deliciously fresh, thanks to zingy salsa and creamy avocado, this is a burger to enjoy when the sun is shining!

    Around 113g beef mince (minimum 20 per cent fat)
    1 brioche burger bun
    Pinch of sea salt and black pepper
    1 egg
    1 tablespoon Burger Sauce (page 224)
    1 Monterey Jack cheese slice
    ½ avocado, sliced
    1 tablespoon Pico de Gallo (page 205)
    French fries, to serve

- Divide the beef mince in two and roll into two balls. Using a sheet of greaseproof paper, flatten the mince into two thin patties. Set aside in the refrigerator for 10 minutes.

- Heat a dry flat frying pan over a medium-high heat. Halve and toast the burger bun face down in the pan for around 30 seconds or until golden. Set aside.

- Place the burger patties onto the hot, dry pan and cook for 1–2 minutes. Flip the burger, add sea salt and black pepper and cook for a further 1 minute or until cooked through and the juices run clear. Set aside to rest.

- Fry the egg in the same pan until the edges are crispy and the yolk is still slightly softened.

- Assemble the burger: Spread Burger Sauce on the bottom burger bun half. Place the cooked California Greening burger on top. Garnish with Monterey Jack cheese, sliced avocado and Pico de Gallo. Top with the fried egg, add the remaining bun half and serve with French fries.

SLOPPY JOE

Serves 3–4

An American classic, Sloppy Joe burgers remove the hassle of shaping patties and flipping whilst cooking, instead offering all the flavour of a good burger and good meatloaf together in a toasted bun.

250g beef mince
1 small onion, peeled and finely chopped
½ green pepper, deseeded and finely chopped
4 tablespoons tomato ketchup
2 teaspoons Worcestershire sauce
¼ teaspoon sea salt
Pinch of black pepper
1 teaspoon soft brown sugar
½ teaspoon yellow (American) mustard
¼ teaspoon paprika
Pinch of garlic powder
50ml water or beef stock
Brioche burger buns and Coleslaw (page 218), to serve

- Heat a wok or large frying pan over a high heat. Add the beef mince to the pan and stir well for 2–3 minutes or until the meat is browned. Drain any excess fat and return the mince to the pan.

- Add the chopped onion and green pepper and stir-fry for a further 2 minutes. Add the tomato ketchup and Worcestershire sauce and mix well. Season and add the brown sugar, yellow mustard, paprika, garlic powder and water or beef stock. Bring to the boil, reduce the heat to low and simmer for around 30 minutes or until thickened.

- Heat a dry, flat frying pan over a medium-high heat. Halve and toast the burger buns face down in the pan for around 30 seconds or until golden. Fill generously with meat and serve with Coleslaw.

PERKED-UP PORK

Serves 1

These pork burgers, essentially homemade sausages, are also excellent as part of a weekend fry-up!

113g pork mince
Pinch of sea salt
Pinch of black pepper
Pinch of caster sugar
1 brioche burger bun
1 teaspoon vegetable oil
1 tablespoon BBQ Sauce, plus extra to serve (page 38)
½ teaspoon sriracha sauce (from supermarkets)
1 tablespoon Coleslaw (page 218)
French fries, to serve

- In a bowl, add pork mince, sea salt, black pepper and sugar. Mix well and roll into a ball.

- Using a sheet of greaseproof paper, flatten the mince into a large patty. Set aside in the refrigerator for 10 minutes.

- Heat a dry flat frying pan over a medium-high heat. Halve and toast the burger bun face down in the pan for around 30 seconds or until golden. Set aside.

- Heat the vegetable oil in the pan over a medium heat. Place the pork patty in the pan and cook for 3–4 minutes or until cooked through and golden, flipping regularly as the burger cooks.

- Assemble the burger: Spread BBQ Sauce and sriracha sauce onto the bottom burger bun. Add the cooked pork patty. Top with Coleslaw and add the remaining burger bun half. Serve with French fries and extra BBQ Sauce on the side.

KOREAN FRIED CHICKEN BURGER

Serves 1

Twice-fried and made using thigh meat, this is the ultimate chicken burger – juicy on the inside and super-crunchy on the outside!

1 boneless, skinless chicken thigh fillet
Pinch of sea salt and black pepper
½ teaspoon rice wine
2–3 tablespoons potato flour or cornflour
Vegetable oil for deep-frying
1 brioche burger bun
Handful of shredded lettuce
1 tablespoon Coleslaw (page 218)

Sauce
¼ teaspoon light soy sauce
¼ teaspoon dark soy sauce
¼ teaspoon Garlic & Ginger Paste (page 228)
1 tablespoon dark brown sugar
½ teaspoon sriracha sauce (from supermarkets)
Pinch of white pepper
Dash of toasted sesame oil

- To make the sauce, add light and dark soy sauces, Garlic & Ginger Paste, dark brown sugar, sriracha sauce, white pepper and toasted sesame oil to a saucepan. Mix well over a low heat and simmer until thickened. Set aside.

- Trim any excess fat from the chicken thigh fillet. Unfold the fillet and sprinkle with sea salt, black pepper and rice wine. Rub the seasoning into the chicken and set aside for 2 minutes. Dredge the chicken fillet in the potato flour or cornflour, shake off any excess and set aside.

- Heat the oil for deep-frying to around 180°C/356°F. Carefully place the breaded chicken thigh fillet in the hot oil. Fry for around 3–4 minutes or until just cooked and slightly crisp. Lift the chicken out of the oil and increase the heat to around 190°C/374°F. Carefully place the fried chicken piece back in the hot oil and fry for a further 1 minute or until the coating is golden and crunchy. Remove from the pan, drain off any excess oil and set aside on kitchen paper.

- Heat a dry flat frying pan over a medium-high heat. Halve and toast the burger bun face down in the pan for around 30 seconds or until golden. Set aside.

- Assemble the burger: Spread the prepared sauce onto the bottom burger bun half. Add the fried chicken. Top with lettuce and Coleslaw, add the remaining burger bun half and serve.

SHREDDED CHICKEN BURGER

Serves 2

Sweet and smoky, this BBQ chicken is equally delicious in tacos or burritos.

1 teaspoon garlic powder
¼ teaspoon ginger powder
¼ teaspoon paprika
½ teaspoon smoked paprika
¼ teaspoon mild chilli powder
1 tablespoon dark brown sugar
½ teaspoon sea salt
¼ teaspoon black pepper
2 skinless, boneless chicken thigh fillets (around 80–90g each)
2 teaspoons vegetable oil
100ml light chicken stock
2 tablespoons BBQ Sauce (page 38)
½ teaspoon sriracha sauce (from supermarkets)
2 brioche burger buns and Coleslaw (page 218), to serve

- In a bowl, add the garlic and ginger powder, paprika, smoked paprika, mild chilli powder, dark brown sugar, sea salt and black pepper. Mix well.

- Coat the chicken pieces with the dry spice rub, cover and set aside in the refrigerator for 1 hour. Remove from the refrigerator 20 minutes before cooking to bring to room temperature.

- Heat the vegetable oil in a large frying pan over a high heat. Add the chicken thighs and fry for 2 minutes or until golden. Flip and cook for a further 2 minutes or until golden on all sides.

- Reduce the heat to low, add the chicken stock and simmer for 7–8 minutes or until the chicken is cooked through (the juices will run clear when pierced with a skewer). Remove the chicken from the pan and transfer to a chopping board. Increase the heat in the pan to high and let the liquid reduce for 2–3 minutes.

- Shred the chicken into very small pieces using two forks or a pair of kitchen scissors. Return the shredded chicken to the pan, increase the heat to high, add the BBQ and sriracha sauces and mix well. Stir-fry the chicken for 2–3 minutes or until the liquid has reduced and the chicken and sauce are sticky.

- Heat a dry flat frying pan over a medium-high heat. Halve and toast the brioche burger buns face down in the pan for around 30 seconds or until golden. Fill generously with shredded chicken and serve with Coleslaw.

BBQ PULLED JACKFRUIT

Serves 4

Perfect for vegetarians but sure to be enjoyed by meat eaters too, jackfruit has the perfect 'pulled pork' consistency when cooked correctly. It is available from Asian and Caribbean grocers.

1 teaspoon garlic powder
¼ teaspoon ginger powder
¼ teaspoon paprika
½ teaspoon smoked paprika
¼ teaspoon mild chilli powder
1 tablespoon dark brown sugar
½ teaspoon sea salt
¼ teaspoon black pepper
2 x 450g tinned jackfruit in water
1 tablespoon vegetable oil
3–4 tablespoons BBQ Sauce (page 38)
50ml light vegetable stock or water
Brioche burger buns, to serve

- In a bowl, add the garlic powder, ginger powder, paprika, smoked paprika, chilli powder, dark brown sugar, sea salt and black pepper. Mix well.

- Drain and rinse the tinned jackfruit and pat dry with kitchen paper. Remove the core and place in a food-safe bowl. Add the prepared spices and mix well.

- Heat the oil in a large frying pan over a medium heat. Add the spiced jackfruit and cook for 2–3 minutes. Add the BBQ Sauce and vegetable stock or water. Mix well, reduce the heat to low and simmer for around 20–30 minutes, breaking up the jackfruit as much as possible with a wooden spoon as it cooks. Increase the heat to high and stir-fry the jackfruit until golden and piping hot.

- Heat a dry flat frying pan over a medium-high heat. Halve and toast the burger buns face down in the pan for around 30 seconds or until golden. Fill generously with pulled jackfruit and serve.

CHILLI CHEESE DOG

Serves 2

An American classic, the chilli added to Cheese Dogs is typically thinner than proper Chilli con Carne and acts almost like a gravy.

½ teaspoon paprika
¼ teaspoon smoked paprika
¼ teaspoon ground coriander powder
½ teaspoon cumin
½ teaspoon chilli powder
½ teaspoon oregano
Pinch of cinnamon
½ teaspoon cocoa powder
Pinch of black pepper
2 teaspoons vegetable oil, plus extra for frying
1 small onion, peeled and finely chopped
1 garlic clove, peeled and crushed
250g minced beef
1 teaspoon tomato ketchup
1 teaspoon Worcestershire sauce
200ml beef stock
2 good-quality pork or beef hot dogs (around 80g weight each)
2 brioche hot dog rolls
2 processed cheese slices

- In a bowl, add the paprika, smoked paprika, coriander, cumin, chilli powder, oregano, cinnamon, cocoa powder and black pepper. Mix well and set aside.

- Heat the vegetable oil in a pan set over a medium heat. Add the onion and cook for 2 minutes. Add the garlic and cook for a further minute. Add the minced beef to the pan and stir well for 2–3 minutes or until the meat is browned. Add the tomato ketchup and Worcestershire sauce and mix well.

- Add the beef stock and prepared spices to the pan. Mix well and heat on high until boiling. Reduce the heat to low and simmer the chilli for around 20 minutes, adding a little water if necessary during cooking. The finished chilli should be on the thin side.

- Fry the hot dogs in a little oil for around 6–7 minutes or until cooked and charred. Meanwhile, preheat the grill on high. When the hot dogs are cooked, slice open the hot dog rolls and place one hot dog inside each roll. Place a cheese slice in the middle, slightly covering both the bread and the hot dog. Place under the grill for 1–2 minutes or until the rolls are warm and slightly toasted and the cheese is melted and bubbling.

- Arrange the hot dogs on serving trays and top generously with the chilli. Serve with extra chilli on the side and lots of napkins.

NACHO DOGS

Serves 2

Topped with fresh Pico de Gallo and zingy, spicy Salsa Verde, these are dogs with a delicious Mexican twist!

Vegetable oil for frying
2 good-quality pork or beef jumbo hot dogs (around 80g weight each)
2 brioche hot dog rolls
2 slices mozzarella cheese
2 tablespoons Salsa Verde, plus extra to serve (page 200)
2 tablespoons Pico de Gallo, plus extra to serve (page 205)

- Heat a little oil in a pan and fry the hot dogs over a medium heat for around 6–7 minutes or until cooked through and slightly charred. Slice open lengthways and fry for a further 30 seconds on the cut side.

- Preheat the grill to high. Slice open the hot dog rolls and place one hot dog inside each. Place a mozzarella cheese slice in the middle, slightly covering both the bread and the hot dog. Place under the grill for 1–2 minutes or until the rolls are warm and slightly toasted and the cheese is melted.

- Arrange the hot dogs on serving trays and top generously with Salsa Verde and Pico de Gallo. Serve with extra Salsa Verde and Pico de Gallo on the side.

DIRTY MAC DOGS

Serves 2

Hot dog? Good. Mac 'n' Cheese? Good. Hot dog smothered in Mac 'n' Cheese? You be the judge . . .

Vegetable oil for frying
2 brioche hot dog rolls
2 good-quality pork or beef jumbo hot dogs (around 80g weight each)
Tomato ketchup, to serve

Mac 'n' Cheese
2 litres of water
Pinch of sea salt
120g macaroni pasta (dry weight)
1 tablespoon salted butter
1 tablespoon plain flour
200ml milk
1 tablespoon mayonnaise
½ teaspoon yellow (American) mustard
Pinch of nutmeg
Pinch of sea salt and black pepper
75g mild or medium Cheddar cheese, grated
15g mozzarella cheese, grated

- In a large saucepan, add the water and sea salt. Bring to the boil, add the dry macaroni pasta and bring back to the boil. Stir once to prevent it from sticking. Simmer for 7–8 minutes or until the pasta is just cooked. Drain and set aside.

- In a small saucepan, heat the butter over a medium-low heat. Once melted, add the flour and mix well until a paste (roux) is formed. Cook out for 1 minute and slowly add the milk, whisking thoroughly.

- Once all of the milk is added, add the mayonnaise, yellow mustard, nutmeg and seasoning. Mix well, stirring constantly over a low heat until the sauce begins to thicken a little. Add the cheeses and cook for a further minute until the cheese has melted and the sauce is thickened. Add the cooked macaroni to the sauce and mix together well to thoroughly coat.

- Heat a touch of oil in a frying pan and fry the hot dogs over a medium heat for around 6–7 minutes or until cooked through and slightly charred.

- Slice the hot dog rolls open down the middle. Place one cooked hot dog inside each roll and top generously with the Mac 'n' Cheese. Top with ketchup and serve with extra Mac 'n' Cheese on the side.

KIMCHI DOGS

Serves 2

These dogs pack quite a punch, perfect for those who like it hot!

Vegetable oil for frying
2 good-quality pork or beef jumbo hot dogs (around 80g weight each)
2 brioche hot dog rolls
2 tablespoons mayonnaise
2 tablespoons Kimchi (page 222)
Sriracha sauce (from supermarkets), to serve

- Heat a touch of oil in a frying pan and fry the hot dogs over a medium heat for around 6–7 minutes or until cooked through and slightly charred.

- Slice the hot dog rolls open down the middle and cover with mayonnaise. Place one cooked hot dog inside each roll, top with Kimchi and serve with sriracha sauce on the side.

CORN DOG BITES

Serves 2

A carnival classic, these hot dog bites are coated in a sweet cornmeal batter.

80g plain flour
60g fine cornmeal
1½ tablespoons caster sugar
½ teaspoon sea salt
½ teaspoon baking powder
1 egg
Just under 100ml semi-skimmed milk
2 good-quality pork or beef jumbo hot dogs (around 80g weight each)
Vegetable oil for deep-frying
1–2 tablespoons plain flour seasoned with sea salt and black pepper
Tomato ketchup and yellow (American) mustard, to serve

- In a large bowl, combine the flour, cornmeal, caster sugar, sea salt, baking powder, egg and milk. Mix thoroughly until the batter becomes thick and smooth.

- Slice each frankfurter hot dog into 4–5 bite-sized pieces. Heat the vegetable oil for deep-frying to around 160°C/320°F.

- Roll each frankfurter piece in the seasoned flour, shaking off any excess. Dunk the floured hot dog pieces in the batter to coat and then place carefully in the hot oil. Turn the corn dog bites occasionally and fry for around 4–5 minutes or until golden.

- Drain off any excess oil and serve the corn dogs with tomato ketchup and mustard.

CURRYWURST

Serves 2

Invented by Herta Heuwer in 1949, this dish has achieved cult status in Germany and can boast fame in the form of the Deutsches Currywurst Museum in Berlin! Topped with a tomato curry sauce that couldn't be simpler in its creation, it's easy to see why this is such a popular snack.

  100ml tomato ketchup
  1 teaspoon mild madras curry powder
  3–4 tablespoons water
  2 teaspoons vegetable oil
  2 good-quality pork or beef jumbo hot dogs (around 80g
      weight per hot dog)

- In a small saucepan, combine the tomato ketchup, curry powder and water. Mix well. Simmer and stir over a medium heat for 3–4 minutes until the spices are combined and the sauce has slightly thickened.

- Heat a touch of vegetable oil in a frying pan set over a medium heat. Fry the hot dogs for around 6–7 minutes or until cooked through and slightly charred. When cooked, cut each dog into 5–6 pieces. Arrange on a serving tray, top with the prepared curry sauce and serve.

VADA PAV (INDIAN POTATO BURGER)

Serves 2

A Mumbai classic, these deep-fried potato patties served in a bread roll with coriander and coconut chutneys are truly delicious! Watch out for the chilli pakoras on the side; they're *hot*!

200g potatoes (2–3 small potatoes)
Sea salt
1 tablespoon vegetable oil, plus extra for deep-frying
¼ teaspoon mustard seeds
2 garlic cloves, peeled and crushed
1 teaspoon grated ginger
2 green chillies, deseeded and finely chopped
¼ teaspoon turmeric
1 teaspoon lemon juice
Handful of fresh coriander leaves, finely chopped
2 soft white bread rolls ('pav')
1 tablespoon Garlic Coconut Chutney (page 234)
1 tablespoon Coriander Chutney (page 235)
2 fresh green chillies
Tomato ketchup, to serve

Batter
100g gram (chickpea) flour (also known as 'besan')
¼ teaspoon turmeric
¼ teaspoon garam masala

Pinch of cumin powder

Pinch of dried fenugreek leaves (also known as 'methi')

¼ teaspoon chilli powder

¼ teaspoon sea salt

Pinch of bicarbonate of soda

Around 100ml water

- Place the potatoes in a saucepan, cover with water, add a pinch of salt and bring to the boil. Simmer for 15–20 minutes or until softened. Drain and mash well; set aside.

- In a frying pan, heat 1 tablespoon of vegetable oil over a medium heat. Add the mustard seeds and gently stir. As the seeds begin to pop with the heat, add garlic, ginger, chopped chillies, turmeric and another pinch of sea salt.

- Add the mashed potato to the frying pan and mix thoroughly to coat. Turn off the heat, sprinkle with lemon juice and coriander leaves and mix once more to combine. Set aside to cool for 30 minutes. At this stage, if you have time the potato mixture may be covered and set aside in the refrigerator overnight for use the next day. This makes preparation easy and allows a more complex flavour to develop in the potato patty.

- In a bowl, combine gram (chickpea) flour, turmeric, garam masala, cumin powder, dried fenugreek, chilli powder, sea salt and bicarbonate of soda. Gradually add around 100ml of water, whisking thoroughly until a smooth, slightly thick batter is created.

- Heat the oil for deep-frying to around 180°C/356°F. Form 4 patties with the spiced potato mixture. Dip each one in the prepared batter to coat and place carefully in the hot oil. Fry the potato pakoras for 3–4 minutes or until golden and crispy. Drain off any excess oil on kitchen paper and set aside to keep warm.

- Use kitchen scissors to cut a slice into the bottom of each green chilli. Dip each one in the pakora batter and place carefully in the hot oil. Fry for 1–2 minutes or until golden.

- Slice open the soft bread rolls ('pav') and cover one half with Garlic Coconut Chutney and the other with Coriander Chutney. Fill with the potato pakoras and serve with chilli pakora and tomato ketchup on the side.

Caution!

Take care when handling fresh chillies and be sure to wash your hands thoroughly after preparing them. For minimal contact, wear gloves or use scissors to slice the chillies whilst handling them carefully by the stem. After preparing fresh chillies, be sure not to scratch any itches without first ensuring your hands are free of heat!

2

RIBS, WINGS & SKEWERS

Cooking over an open flame is perhaps the original and best way to cook. In countries all around the world, different meats and spice mixes offer variety to what are essentially dishes of pure simplicity, good-quality meat grilled until smoky and slightly charred. The aroma of barbecued meats and vegetables is part of the heady atmosphere which exists at street food festivals and busy city locations, attracting customers from far and wide.

If you're lucky enough to have the equipment (and the weather!) to cook outdoors, the recipes included in this chapter will work fantastically well on a charcoal BBQ. Adjust cooking times accordingly, or cook using the specified methods/times and finish on an outdoor BBQ for just a few minutes to add flavour and authenticity.

For indoor cooking, modern-day health grills produce excellent results when cooking kebabs and skewered foods. Cooking times should be halved when using these grills as both sides cook simultaneously. Another added bonus to using a health grill to cook your skewers is that the clean drip tray is the perfect shape and size for soaking wooden skewers before cooking!

KALBI KUI (KOREAN RIBS)

Serves 2

Also known as Galbi Kui, these ribs are flavoured with mirin, a rice wine similar to sake but with a slightly sweeter finish. The dish uses flanken-style short ribs, which your butcher will be able to prepare for you.

1.2kg flanken-style short ribs
Sesame seeds and finely chopped spring onions, to serve

Marinade
4 large garlic cloves, peeled and roughly chopped
1 teaspoon grated ginger
3 tablespoons light soy sauce
3 tablespoons dark soy sauce
2 tablespoons mirin
2 teaspoons sesame oil
1 tablespoon rice wine vinegar
3–4 tablespoons water
3 tablespoons soft brown sugar
2 spring onions, trimmed, peeled and roughly chopped
Pinch of black pepper
Pinch of white pepper

- To make the marinade, add the garlic cloves, ginger, soy sauces, mirin, sesame oil, rice wine vinegar, water, sugar, roughly chopped spring onions and peppers to the bowl of a blender. Blend until smooth.

- Arrange the ribs in a food-safe container and pour over the marinade. Mix well and set aside in the refrigerator for 4–6 hours, occasionally turning the ribs in the marinade.

- Preheat a ridged griddle pan over a medium-high heat. Arrange the ribs on a rack, discarding the excess marinade. Cook the ribs for 3–4 minutes on each side until slightly charred and cooked through (the juices will run clear when pierced with a skewer).

- Meanwhile, toast the sesame seeds. Heat a wok or large frying pan over a medium heat. Add the sesame seeds and dry roast for 2–3 minutes or until slightly browned and aromatic.

- Arrange the ribs on a serving plate and top with finely chopped spring onions and toasted sesame seeds.

BBQ RIBS

Serves 2

If you're lucky enough to have the weather for it, these ribs can be finished off on an outdoor BBQ with excellent results.

2 large pork rib racks (each around 700g in weight)
200ml water
500ml cola

BBQ Sauce
100ml tomato ketchup
1 tablespoon sweet chilli sauce
1 tablespoon sriracha sauce (from supermarkets)
1 tablespoon Worcestershire sauce
1 tablespoon light soy sauce
1 tablespoon dark soy sauce
½ teaspoon oregano
½ teaspoon paprika
½ teaspoon smoked paprika
½ teaspoon garlic powder
4 tablespoons soft brown sugar
Pinch of black pepper

- To make the sauce place the tomato ketchup, sweet chilli sauce, sriracha sauce, Worcestershire sauce, light and dark soy sauces, oregano, paprika, smoked paprika, garlic powder, sugar and black pepper in a bowl. Mix well, cover and set aside.

- Meanwhile preheat the oven to 160°C/Gas 3. Arrange the ribs in a roasting tray and pour water and cola over the top. Cover with two layers of foil and place in the centre of the oven for 1 hour and 20 minutes.

- Remove the tray from the oven, peel back the foil and turn the ribs over. Cover again, return to the oven and cook for a further hour and 20 minutes. Remove the cooked ribs from the oven, drain off the liquid and set aside on a plate or baking tray to cool.

- Once cool, arrange the ribs in a food-safe container. Cover with the prepared sauce and mix well. Cover and refrigerate for at least 4 hours or, ideally, overnight.

- When ready to eat, preheat the oven to 220°C/Gas 7. Arrange the ribs on a baking tray, place in the centre of the oven and cook for 15–20 minutes, basting occasionally with sauce and turning.

- When the ribs are piping hot, sticky and crispy, remove from the oven and set aside on a board to rest for 2 minutes to allow the meat to firm up. Slice into individual ribs and serve.

SWEET & SPICY RIBS

Serves 2

Spicy, sticky and sweet, these ribs will bake happily in the oven to accompany your favourite Thai dishes.

1.4kg pork ribs
Toasted sesame seeds (page 37) and 1–2 spring onions, trimmed, peeled and finely sliced, to serve

Marinade
4 tablespoons hoisin sauce
2 tablespoons oyster sauce
1 teaspoon light soy sauce
2 teaspoons dark soy sauce
1 tablespoon clear honey
1 tablespoon rice wine vinegar
1 tablespoon rice wine
2 teaspoons toasted sesame oil
2 teaspoons Chinese five-spice
Pinch each of black and white pepper

- To make the marinade, in a bowl, place the hoisin sauce, oyster sauce, light and dark soy sauces, honey, rice wine vinegar, rice wine, toasted sesame oil, Chinese five-spice, black and white pepper. Mix well.

- Preheat the oven to 160°C/Gas 3. Meanwhile arrange the ribs in a large dish and cover with half the marinade, reserving the remainder for basting as the ribs cook. Pour the marinade evenly around all of the ribs. Arrange the ribs on a roasting tray, cover loosely with foil and place in the centre of the oven. Bake for 1 hour.

- Remove the roasting tray from the oven, peel back the foil and turn the ribs over. Brush with more marinade and return to the oven, this time uncovered. Bake for a further 40 minutes, turning and basting with more sauce occasionally until the ribs are tender and glazed (the juices should run clear when pierced with a skewer).

- Remove the roasting tray from the oven and set the ribs aside to rest and firm up for 5 minutes. Arrange on a serving plate and top with toasted sesame seeds and spring onions.

SRIRACHA BUFFALO WINGS

Serves 4

For extra-crispy wings, try lightly breading them in seasoned flour and deep-frying for 7–8 minutes in hot vegetable oil.

Around 1kg chicken wings, jointed and wing tips removed (your butcher can do this for you)
¼ teaspoon sea salt
Pinch of black pepper
1 teaspoon vegetable oil
Pinch of dried parsley, to serve

Sauce
3 tablespoons salted butter
3 tablespoons sriracha sauce (from supermarkets)
Pinch of garlic powder

- Preheat the oven to 200°C/Gas 6. Meanwhile in a small bowl, combine the salted butter, sriracha sauce and garlic powder. Cover and set aside.

- Arrange the chicken wings on a wire rack above a baking tray (this will ensure the wings are crispy on all sides). For easy clean up, line the baking tray with foil. Rub the seasoning into the chicken wings and let stand for 2 minutes. Rub the oil into the wings and place in the centre of the oven.

Bake for around 35 minutes or until cooked and crispy (the juices will run clear when pierced with a skewer), turning occasionally.

• When the wings are almost cooked, heat the prepared butter and sriracha sauce mixture in a saucepan set over a medium heat for 2–3 minutes until slightly thickened. Pour the sauce into a large food-safe bowl and add the cooked chicken wings. Mix thoroughly until evenly coated in sauce.

• Arrange the chicken wings on a serving plate, sprinkle with dried parsley and serve.

JAMAICAN JERK WINGS

Serves 4

Made using exceptionally hot scotch bonnet chillies, these wings pack a punch! Whilst proper chilli preparation etiquette should be followed in any case (see page 33), this advice is particularly pertinent here.

1.2kg chicken wings, jointed and wing tips removed (your butcher can do this for you)

Marinade
1–2 scotch bonnet chillies, deseeded
3 large garlic cloves, peeled
2 spring onions, trimmed, peeled and roughly chopped
½ small red onion, peeled and roughly chopped
1 tablespoon dark brown sugar
1 tablespoon light soy sauce
2 teaspoons dark soy sauce
½ teaspoon allspice
¼ teaspoon paprika
¼ teaspoon smoked paprika
Pinch of cinnamon
Pinch of nutmeg
Pinch of cumin powder
¼ teaspoon dried mixed herbs
3 tablespoons lime juice
2 tablespoons vegetable oil

- To the bowl of a blender add the deseeded scotch bonnet chillies, garlic, spring onions, red onion, sugar, soy sauces, allspice, paprika, smoked paprika, cinnamon, nutmeg, cumin powder, dried mixed herbs, lime juice and vegetable oil. Blend thoroughly until the marinade is smooth.

- Arrange the chicken wings in a food-safe container. Cover with around half of the marinade, reserving the remainder for basting as the wings cool. Mix well with a wooden spoon or spatula until all the wings are coated. Cover and set aside in the refrigerator for at least 4 hours or, ideally, over-night. Remove from the refrigerator 30 minutes before cooking.

- Meanwhile preheat the oven to 200°C/Gas 6. Arrange the chicken wings on a wire rack above a baking tray (this will ensure the wings are crispy on all sides). For easy clean up, line the baking tray with foil. Discard any leftover mari-nade covering the raw chicken.

- Bake for around 25 minutes or until the chicken wings are golden and crispy (the juices should run clear when pierced with a skewer). Brush generously with the remaining mari-nade and return to the oven for a further 20–25 minutes, turning and basting with more sauce every few minutes.

- Arrange the chicken wings on a serving plate and serve.

SUYA (NIGERIAN BEEF SKEWERS) WITH STREET SALAD

Serves 2

Also known as 'Tsitsinga', these beef skewers are deliciously nutty and perfect served with a fresh salad on the side.

½ chicken stock cube, crumbled
½ teaspoon paprika
½ teaspoon smoked paprika
1 teaspoon garlic powder
¼ teaspoon ginger powder
1 teaspoon onion powder
½ teaspoon white pepper
½ teaspoon cayenne pepper
Pinch of chilli powder
1 tablespoon roasted salted peanuts
2 sirloin steaks (each around 250g weight)
2 tablespoons vegetable oil
Lemon slices, to serve

Street salad
2 salad tomatoes, deseeded and roughly chopped
½ red cabbage, finely sliced
1 red onion, peeled and finely sliced
½ cucumber, peeled, deseeded and finely sliced
2 tablespoons lemon juice
2 teaspoons extra virgin olive oil

Pinch of sea salt
Pinch of black pepper

- In a bowl, place the chicken stock cube and all the spices. Mix well and set aside.

- Put the roasted peanuts in the bowl of a blender or spice grinder and grind to a fine powder. Add to the spice mix.

- Slice each sirloin steak into 5–6 thin strips. Place in a food-safe container and sprinkle with the dry spices and peanuts. Rub the mix thoroughly into the meat, cover and set aside at room temperature for 30 minutes. Add the vegetable oil and mix.

- Thirty minutes before cooking, soak some wooden skewers in water to ensure they don't burn.

- Preheat the grill to medium-hot. Meanwhile ribbon beef strips onto the soaked wooden skewers, ensuring each piece is pierced several times by the skewer (each skewer should comfortably hold 2–3 beef strips). Repeat the process until all of the meat is arranged on the skewers.

- Cook the skewers of meat under the grill for around 10–12 minutes, turning occasionally until cooked through and slightly charred (the juices should run clear when pierced with a skewer). Alternatively, grill on a double-plated health grill for 5–6 minutes.

- Whilst the meat cooks, mix all the salad ingredients together in a bowl.

- Arrange the cooked Suya skewers on a serving plate, garnish with lemon slices and serve with the Street Salad.

MOO PING (THAI GRILLED PORK SKEWERS)

Serves 2

Utterly addictive sweet and salty pork skewers made tender with potato flour and coconut milk. Often made with coriander roots, stems provide a good alternative.

450g pork loin fillet
1 teaspoon potato flour or cornflour
50ml coconut milk, plus extra for brushing
8 wooden skewers
Fresh coriander leaves, finely chopped, and Thai Sticky
  Rice (page 169), to serve

Marinade
2 garlic cloves, peeled
Handful of fresh coriander stems, chopped
Pinch of white pepper
Pinch of sea salt
1 tablespoon oyster sauce
2 teaspoons light soy sauce
2 teaspoons dark soy sauce
1 teaspoon dark brown sugar

- In a pestle and mortar, combine the garlic, coriander stems, white pepper and sea salt. Bash and grind until well combined. Transfer to a bowl and add the oyster sauce, light and dark soy sauces and sugar.

- Trim any excess fat from the pork loin and cut into thin strips. Place in a food-safe container and pour over the marinade. Mix thoroughly to coat, cover and set aside in the refrigerator for at least 4 hours, or ideally, overnight.

- Thirty minutes before cooking, soak the wooden skewers in water to ensure they don't burn and remove the marinated pork from the refrigerator.

- Preheat the grill to medium-hot. Meanwhile add the potato flour or cornflour and coconut milk to the marinated pork. Mix well to combine and ribbon each pork strip onto the pre-soaked skewers, ensuring each piece is pierced several times by the skewer (each skewer should comfortably hold 2–3 pork strips). Repeat the process until all of the meat is arranged on the skewers.

- Cook the skewers under the grill for around 10–12 minutes, turning, until cooked through and slightly charred (the juices should run clear when pierced with a skewer). Alternatively, grill on a double-plated health grill for 5–6 minutes. As the pork grills, turn the skewers occasionally and brush with a little extra coconut milk.

- When the Moo Ping skewers are ready, arrange on a serving plate and serve garnished with fresh coriander and Thai Sticky Rice.

YANG ROU CHUAN (CHINESE LAMB KEBABS)

Serves 2

Beijing-style lamb kebabs, these skewered meats are undoubtedly amongst the most popular of Chinese street foods.

300g lamb leg or shoulder
8 wooden skewers
Fresh coriander, finely chopped, to serve

Marinade
1 tablespoon vegetable oil
1 teaspoon cumin powder
¼ teaspoon garlic powder
½ teaspoon dried crushed chillies
¼ teaspoon Sichuan pepper
Pinch of Chinese Five-spice
¼ teaspoon sea salt
¼ teaspoon black pepper
1 teaspoon rice wine

- In a food-safe bowl, combine the vegetable oil, cumin powder, garlic powder, chillies, Sichuan pepper, Chinese Five-spice, sea salt, black pepper and rice wine. Mix well.

- Trim any excess fat from the lamb, leaving a little on for flavour. Cut the lamb into thin strips and add to the marinade. Mix well, cover and set aside in the refrigerator for at least 2 hours, or ideally, overnight.

- Thirty minutes before cooking, soak the wooden skewers in water to ensure they don't burn and remove the marinated pork from the refrigerator.

- Preheat the grill to medium-hot. Meanwhile ribbon each lamb strip onto the pre-soaked skewers, ensuring each piece is pierced several times by the skewer (each skewer should comfortably hold 2–3 lamb strips). Repeat the process until all of the meat is arranged on the skewers.

- Cook the skewers under the grill for around 10–12 minutes until cooked through and slightly charred (the juices should run clear when pierced with a skewer). Alternatively, grill on a double-plated health grill for 5–6 minutes, turning occasionally. Arrange on a serving plate, garnish with fresh coriander and serve.

DAKKOCHI (KOREAN GRILLED CHICKEN SKEWERS)

Serves 2

This marinade is usually made using Asian pears. If you're lucky enough to find them (they can occasionally be sourced at larger fruit and vegetable markets or via specialist online stores), by all means use in place of the pineapple juice in this recipe.

- 4 skinless, boneless chicken breast fillets (each around 113g weight)
- 8 wooden skewers
- 1–2 spring onions, trimmed, peeled and finely chopped, and Thai Sticky Rice (page 169), to serve

Marinade

2 large cloves garlic, peeled and crushed

1 teaspoon grated ginger

½ small onion, peeled and very finely chopped

2 teaspoons light soy sauce

2 teaspoons dark soy sauce

1 tablespoon dark brown sugar

Pinch each of black and white pepper

1 teaspoon toasted sesame oil

4 tablespoons pineapple juice

1 tablespoon rice wine

- In a bowl, combine the garlic, ginger, onion, light and dark soy sauces, sugar, black and white peppers, toasted sesame oil, pineapple juice and rice wine. Mix well and reserve a little of the marinade in a separate bowl for basting.

- Trim any excess fat from the chicken breasts and cut each fillet into 5–6 thin strips. Place in a food-safe container and pour over the marinade. Mix thoroughly to coat, cover and set aside in the refrigerator for 2 hours.

- Thirty minutes before cooking, soak the wooden skewers in water to ensure they don't burn and remove the marinated chicken from the refrigerator.

- Preheat the grill to medium-hot. Meanwhile ribbon each chicken strip onto the pre-soaked skewers, ensuring each piece is pierced several times by the skewer (each skewer should comfortably hold 2–3 chicken strips). Repeat the process until all of the meat is arranged on the skewers. Discard any leftover marinade that has been in contact with the raw chicken.

- Cook the skewers under the grill for around 10–12 minutes until cooked through and slightly charred (the juices should run clear when pierced with a skewer). Alternatively, grill on a double-plated health grill for 5–6 minutes. As the chicken grills, turn the skewers occasionally and brush with the reserved marinade.

- When the Dakkochi skewers are ready, arrange on a serving plate and garnish with finely chopped spring onions. Serve with Thai Sticky Rice.

SRIRACHA SOY & LIME SKEWERS

Serves 2

This simple marinade adds great flavour without overpowering the chicken, which remains the star of the show in these spicy-sweet skewers.

4–6 skinless, boneless chicken thigh fillets (around 450g total weight)

8 wooden skewers

1 lime, cut into 8 wedges, to serve

Marinade

1 garlic clove, peeled and crushed

½ teaspoon grated ginger

1 teaspoon light soy sauce

1 teaspoon dark soy sauce

Pinch of cumin powder

¼ teaspoon potato flour or cornflour

2 teaspoons sriracha sauce (from supermarkets)

2 teaspoons vegetable oil

1 teaspoon clear honey

Zest and juice of ½ lime

- In a bowl, combine the garlic, ginger, light and dark soy sauces, cumin powder, potato flour or cornflour, sriracha sauce, vegetable oil, honey, lime zest and juice. Mix well.

- Trim any excess fat from the chicken thighs and cut each fillet into 3–4 thin strips. Place in a food-safe container and pour over the marinade. Mix thoroughly, cover and set aside in the refrigerator for 4 hours, or ideally, overnight.

- Thirty minutes before cooking, soak the wooden skewers in water to ensure they don't burn and remove the marinated chicken from the refrigerator. Preheat the grill to medium-hot. Meanwhile ribbon each chicken strip onto the pre-soaked skewers, ensuring each piece is pierced several times by the skewer (each skewer should comfortably hold 2–3 chicken strips). Repeat the process until all of the meat is arranged on the skewers. Discard any leftover marinade that has been in contact with the raw chicken.

- Cook the skewers under the grill for around 10–12 minutes until cooked through and slightly charred (the juices should run clear when pierced with a skewer). Alternatively, grill on a double-plated health grill for 5-6 minutes, turning occasionally. Arrange on a plate and serve with lime wedges.

YAKITON (JAPANESE GRILLED PORK SKEWERS)

Serves 2

Grilled pork skewers, packed full of flavour with just a few simple ingredients and seasoned with a Japanese spice mix known as shichimi, which includes chilli pepper, orange peel, sesame seeds and ginger. Shichimi is available from Chinese supermarkets or specialist online stores. It's also available in some larger traditional supermarkets.

450g pork loin fillet
1 teaspoon potato flour or cornflour
8 wooden skewers
Pinch of shichimi, to serve

Marinade
50ml light soy sauce
50ml dark soy sauce
40ml mirin (see also page 36)
1 tablespoon sake
3 tablespoons dark brown sugar
1 large garlic clove, peeled

- In a saucepan place the soy sauces, mirin, sake, sugar and garlic clove. Set over high heat and bring to the boil, then reduce the heat to low and simmer for 5–6 minutes or until the marinade begins to foam and reduce. Remove the garlic and set aside.

- Trim any excess fat from the pork loin and slice into 20–24 thin strips. Place in a food-safe container and add 2 table-spoons of the prepared sauce. Mix thoroughly, cover and set aside for 5 minutes.

- Thirty minutes before cooking, soak the wooden skewers in water to ensure they don't burn.

- Preheat the grill to medium-hot. Meanwhile add the potato flour or cornflour to the marinated pork. Mix well and ribbon each pork strip onto the pre-soaked skewers, ensuring each piece is pierced several times by the skewer (each skewer should comfortably hold 2–3 pork strips). Repeat the process until all of the meat is arranged on the skewers. Discard any excess marinade which has been in contact with the pork.

- Cook the skewers under the grill for around 10–12 minutes until cooked through and slightly charred (the juices should run clear when pierced with a skewer). Alternatively, grill on a double-plated health grill for 5–6 minutes. Brush a little excess marinade onto the skewers and turn as they are cooking.

- Arrange the cooked Yakiton skewers on a serving plate, garnish with shichimi and serve.

INIHAW NA MANOK (FILIPINO GRILLED CHICKEN)

Serves 2

As soon as you start grilling these sweet and slightly spicy skewers and the aroma fills the air, you know you're on to a good thing!

- 4–6 skinless, boneless chicken thigh fillets (around 450g weight)
- 8 wooden skewers
- Handful of fresh coriander leaves, finely chopped, to serve

Marinade
- 1½ teaspoons light soy sauce
- 1½ teaspoons dark soy sauce
- 1 tablespoon lime juice
- 1 tablespoon soft brown sugar
- 1 tablespoon tomato ketchup
- 1 teaspoon sriracha sauce (from supermarkets)
- 50ml Sprite or 7UP
- ½ teaspoon sesame oil
- Pinch of sea salt
- Pinch of black pepper
- Pinch of white pepper
- Pinch of garlic powder

- In a bowl, combine the light and dark soy sauces, lime juice, sugar, ketchup, sriracha sauce, Sprite or 7UP, sesame oil, sea salt, black pepper, white pepper and garlic powder. Mix well and reserve a little of the marinade in a separate bowl for basting. Cover both bowls and set aside.

- Trim any excess fat from the chicken thighs and cut each fillet into 3–4 strips. Place in a food-safe container and pour over the marinade. Mix thoroughly to coat and set aside in the refrigerator for 2 hours.

- Thirty minutes before cooking, soak the wooden skewers in water to ensure they don't burn and remove the marinated chicken from the refrigerator.

- Preheat the grill to medium-hot. Meanwhile ribbon each chicken strip onto the pre-soaked skewers, ensuring each piece is pierced several times by the skewer (each skewer should comfortably hold 2–3 chicken strips). Repeat the process until all of the meat is arranged on the skewers. Discard any leftover marinade which has been in contact with the raw chicken.

- Cook the skewers under the grill for around 10–12 minutes until cooked through and slightly charred (the juices should run clear when pierced with a skewer). Alternatively, grill on a double-plated health grill for 5–6 minutes. As the chicken grills, turn the skewers occasionally and brush with the reserved marinade.

- When the Inihaw na Manok is ready, arrange on a serving plate, garnish with fresh coriander and serve.

59

VEGETABLE STREET SKEWERS

Serves 2

These vegetable skewers are perfect for vegetarian guests or served alongside any kebabs or grilled meats. It's always best to prepare them separately from meat skewers as the cooking times often differ.

10–12 small button mushrooms
1 large red onion, peeled
1 pepper (or a mix of yellow, red and green)
1 courgette
8 wooden skewers

Marinade
2 tablespoons olive oil
2 tablespoons lemon juice
½ teaspoon garlic powder
¼ teaspoon cumin powder
¼ teaspoon paprika
Pinch of smoked paprika
Pinch of cayenne pepper
Pinch of dried parsley
¼ teaspoon sea salt
¼ teaspoon black pepper

- In a bowl, place the olive oil, lemon juice, garlic powder, cumin powder, paprika, smoked paprika, cayenne pepper, dried parsley, sea salt and black pepper. Mix thoroughly, cover and set aside.

- Thirty minutes before cooking, soak the wooden skewers in water to ensure they don't burn.

- Preheat the grill to medium-hot. Meanwhile peel the mushrooms and chop the onion into bite-sized wedges. Rinse the pepper and courgette and pat dry with kitchen paper. Cut into large bite-sized pieces, removing seeds from the pepper, and arrange on the pre-soaked skewers. Brush the skewers generously with the prepared marinade, reserving a little for basting during cooking.

- Cook the skewers under the grill for around 10–12 minutes until cooked through and slightly charred. Alternatively, grill on a double-plated health grill for 5–6 minutes. Brush a little extra marinade onto the skewers as they are cooking and keep turning.

- Arrange the cooked vegetable skewers on a serving plate and serve hot alongside kebabs, wraps or grilled meats.

3

TACOS, WRAPS &
SANDWICHES

Where Mexico has its tacos, India has its chapati breads, France and Vietnam have their crispy baguettes, and the UK and India have their traditional white bread rolls or 'pav'. Wrapping things in bread is popular worldwide and, of course, offers a perfect delivery system for street food, the bread acting as a hand-held wrapper for the delicious fillings inside.

Tortilla baskets are available online from specialist Mexican grocers and are ideal for keeping tortillas warm. Alternatively, wrap tortillas in a clean tea towel until ready for use. Virgin olive oil is ideal for marinades or for use in cooking. Extra virgin oil should be used exclusively for salad dressings as the flavour is lost somewhat in the cooking process.

If your only experience of Mexican tacos is those crunchy deep-fried shells purchased in boxes at the supermarket, soft corn tacos will change your life. Made using masa harina (literally translated as 'dough flour', a finely ground cornmeal), the fragrant and sweet flavour of a soft corn tortilla is hard to beat. For coeliacs, it doesn't hurt of course that corn tortillas are gluten-free into the bargain.

From crispy Hungarian Langos or Fried Bread, smothered in garlic butter to soft bread rolls piled high with roasted pork, this chapter includes all manner of bread and bread-type dishes perfect for wrapping, folding and tearing. Bring on the bread!

BREAKFAST TACOS

Serves 1

These are prepared in minutes and are the perfect pick-me-up. For an added indulgence, slip in some crispy fried chorizo.

½ teaspoon butter

2 eggs

Pinch of salt and black pepper

6 small soft corn tortillas

2 teaspoons mayonnaise

2 tablespoons Salsa Verde (page 200) or sriracha sauce
   (from supermarkets)

2 tablespoons Pico de Gallo (page 205)

- In a small saucepan set over a medium heat, mix the butter and eggs together. Scramble the eggs, seasoning just as they finish cooking. Set aside and keep warm.

- Toast the tortillas in a dry pan over a medium-high heat for 20–30 seconds each side. As the tortillas are toasted, wrap them in a clean tea towel or place in a tortilla basket to keep warm.

- Overlap the tortillas in twos on a serving plate. Brush each one with a little mayonnaise and top with scrambled egg. Spoon over the Salsa Verde or sriracha sauce and finally top with Pico de Gallo just before serving.

TACOS CARNITAS

Serves 8

Literally translated as 'little meats', carnitas meat is crispy, salty and sweet all at once.

2.1kg boneless pork shoulder
2 teaspoons vegetable oil, plus extra for frying
2 large garlic cloves, peeled and crushed
1 small onion, peeled and finely chopped
1 green jalapeño pepper, deseeded and finely chopped
    (see also page 33)
150ml smooth orange juice
1 bay leaf
6 small soft corn tortillas per person to serve
Pico de Gallo (page 205), Salsa Verde (page 200) and
    sliced red radishes, to serve

Spice Mix
2 teaspoons cumin
¼ teaspoon coriander powder
Pinch of cinnamon
¼ teaspoon garlic powder
2 teaspoons Mexican oregano (see Box page 68)
1½ teaspoons sea salt
¼ teaspoon black pepper

- In a bowl, add cumin, coriander powder, cinnamon, garlic powder, oregano, sea salt and black pepper. Mix well. Rub the spice mix all around the pork shoulder and set aside for 5 minutes. Add 2 teaspoons vegetable oil and rub all over until the pork is evenly coated.

- Place the pork shoulder in a slow cooker. Add the garlic, onion, jalapeño, orange juice and bay leaf. Cook on low for 8–9 hours. Alternatively, the carnitas may be cooked in a regular oven preheated to 160°C/Gas 3 for 5 hours.

- Remove the pork from the slow cooker and set aside to rest for 15 minutes. Pour the remaining liquid from the slow cooker into a saucepan and reduce over a medium heat, stirring, for 3–4 minutes. Transfer to a food-safe container and set aside to cool.

- Shred the pork using two forks or clean hands. At this stage the pork can be finished immediately or set aside in the refrigerator for up to 24 hours. When ready to eat, heat 1–2 teaspoons vegetable oil in a frying pan over a medium-high heat. Put the shredded meat in the pan and mix well. Cook for 2 minutes, stirring occasionally.

- Press and flatten the pork in the pan and cook, untouched, for a further 2 minutes or until the pork at the bottom of the pan is crispy and sizzling. As the pork cooks, add 2–3 teaspoons of the reserved cooking juice.

- Toast the soft corn tortillas in a dry frying pan set over a medium-high heat for around 20–30 seconds on each side. As the tortillas are toasted, wrap them in a clean tea towel or place in a tortilla basket to keep warm.

- Overlap the tortillas in twos on a serving plate. Top with the carnitas, Pico de Gallo, Salsa Verde and sliced radishes and serve.

Note

Mexican oregano is available online from specialist Mexican grocers. Oregano from your local supermarket will provide a suitable alternative.

TACOS AL PASTOR (PORK & PINEAPPLE TACOS)

Serves 4

It's the achiote paste (also known as annatto paste) in this marinade which gives the pork its deliciously vibrant red colour, as well as adding a slightly earthy flavour. The fresh pineapple garnish adds a burst of flavour. For added sweetness, dust the pineapple chunks with a little sugar and chargrill briefly before serving.

4 pork chops (around 200g weight each)
1½ teaspoons sea salt
100ml light chicken stock
24 small soft corn tortillas (6 per person)
1 tablespoon Onion & Coriander Salsa (page 221), fresh
    pineapple chunks and Salsa Verde (page 200), to serve

Marinade
1 dried ancho chilli (see Box page 71)
1 tablespoon achiote paste
1 tablespoon distilled white vinegar
4 garlic cloves
1 jalapeño chilli (see also page 33)
½ teaspoon cumin powder
¼ teaspoon smoked paprika
1 teaspoon Mexican oregano (see page 68)
¼ teaspoon allspice

Pinch of mild chilli powder
½ teaspoon chipotle chilli flakes
Pinch of black pepper
2 tablespoons water
2 tablespoons vegetable oil

- Heat a dry frying pan over a medium heat. De-stem and deseed the dried ancho chilli. Toast for around 1–2 minutes or until a slightly nutty aroma fills the air. Place in a bowl and cover with boiling water. Set aside for 15 minutes, drain off the water and the chilli is ready for use. Alternatively, the chilli may be cold-soaked: simply cover with water and set aside for 10–12 hours.

- In a small bowl, mix the achiote paste and vinegar.

- In a blender, combine the soaked chilli, achiote paste and vinegar, garlic, jalapeño, cumin powder, smoked paprika, oregano, allspice, chilli powder, chipotle chilli flakes, black pepper, water and vegetable oil. Blend into a smooth paste, adding just a touch more water or vegetable oil if necessary.

- Trim any excess fat from the pork chops, leaving a generous amount on for flavour. Arrange in a food-safe container and cover with the marinade. Mix well and set aside in the refrigerator for 4 hours, or ideally, overnight.

- Thirty minutes before cooking, remove the marinated pork from the refrigerator. Add the sea salt and mix thoroughly to combine.

- Heat a large frying pan over a medium-high heat. Carefully place the marinated pork chops inside and fry for 3–4 minutes on each side. Add the chicken stock, reduce the heat to low and simmer for a further 7–8 minutes or until cooked through. Remove from the pan, increase the heat to high and allow the liquid to reduce.

- Slice the pork chops into small bite-sized pieces. Return to the pan, increase the heat to high and stir-fry for 1–2 minutes or until charred and piping hot.

- Meanwhile toast the soft corn tortillas in a dry pan set over a medium-high heat for around 20–30 seconds on each side. As the tortillas are toasted, wrap them in a clean tea towel or place in a tortilla basket to keep warm.

- Overlap the tortillas in twos on a serving plate. Arrange the pork on top. Garnish with Onion & Coriander Salsa, fresh pineapple chunks and Salsa Verde.

A Note on Chillies

Ancho chillies are dried poblano chillies, which are mild but full of flavour. Originating in Puebla, Mexico, the dried chillies are available online from specialist Mexican grocers and also from larger supermarkets.

BEEF TACOS

Serves 4

This smoky, spicy Mexican Beef also makes a perfect topping for Nachos (page 199).

500g beef mince
250ml beef stock
24 small soft corn tortillas (6 per person)
Sour cream, Pico de Gallo (page 205) and Salsa Verde
   (page 200), to serve

Spice Mix
1 teaspoon cornflour
1 teaspoon garlic powder
½ teaspoon onion powder
2 teaspoons dried onion flakes
1 teaspoon cumin powder
½ teaspoon paprika
1 teaspoon smoked paprika
½ teaspoon Mexican oregano (see page 68)
Pinch of cayenne pepper
Pinch of chilli powder
Pinch of sea salt
¼ teaspoon black pepper
¼ teaspoon white pepper

- In a small bowl, combine the cornflour, garlic and onion powders, dried onion flakes, cumin powder, paprika, smoked paprika, Mexican oregano, cayenne pepper, chilli powder, sea salt, black pepper and white pepper. Mix well.

- Heat a large frying pan over a medium-high heat. Place the beef mince inside the pan and brown for 2–3 minutes, stirring and breaking up the mince. When browned, drain off any excess fat. Add the prepared spice mix and stir well for 30 seconds. Add the beef stock, bring to boiling and reduce the heat to medium-low. Let the taco beef simmer for 15–20 minutes, stirring occasionally until the meat begins to dry up in the pan.

- Towards the end of cooking time toast the soft corn tortillas in a dry frying pan set over a medium-high heat for around 30–40 seconds on each side. As the tortillas are toasted, wrap them in a clean tea towel or place in a tortilla basket to keep warm.

- Arrange the tortillas in twos on a warmed serving plate. Spread a little sour cream on each tortilla, top with the taco beef, Pico de Gallo and Salsa Verde and serve.

TACOS DE POLLO (SHREDDED CHICKEN TACOS)

Serves 4

Smoky, spicy and full of flavour, using chicken thighs ensures that the chicken remains juicy, even after being crisped up in the pan. Perhaps my favourite tacos, crying out to be smothered with Pico de Gallo and Salsa Verde.

4–6 skinless, boneless chicken thigh fillets (around 450g total weight)

100ml light chicken stock

24 small soft corn tacos (6 per person)

Sour cream, Pico de Gallo and Salsa Verde (page 205 and 200), to serve

Marinade

1 dried ancho chilli (see page 71)

½ red onion, peeled and roughly chopped

2 garlic cloves, peeled

½ teaspoon cumin powder

½ teaspoon paprika

½ teaspoon smoked paprika

½ teaspoon mild chilli powder

½ teaspoon chipotle chilli flakes (optional but recommended)

1 teaspoon chipotle in adobo (available in tins or jars online from specialist Mexican grocers)

2 tablespoons lime juice

2 tablespoons virgin olive oil

2 tablespoons water

½ teaspoon salt

Pinch of black pepper

- Heat a dry frying pan over a medium heat. De-stem and deseed the ancho chilli. Toast the dried ancho chilli for around 1–2 minutes or until a slightly nutty aroma fills the air. Place in a bowl and cover with boiling water. Set aside for 15 minutes, drain off the water and the chilli is ready for use. Alternatively, the chilli may be 'cold soaked' for 10–12 hours in cold water.

- In a blender, combine the soaked chilli, red onion, garlic, cumin, paprika, smoked paprika, chilli powder, chipotle chilli flakes (if using), chipotle in adobo, lime juice, olive oil and water. Blend to a smooth paste, adding just a touch more water or oil, if necessary.

- Arrange the chicken in a food-safe container and cover with the marinade. Set aside in the refrigerator for 4 hours, or ideally, overnight. Remove the chicken from the refrigerator 30 minutes before cooking. Heat a frying pan over a medium-high heat. Lift the chicken out of the marinade and allow excess to drip off. Place the chicken thighs in the frying pan and cook on one side, untouched, for 2 minutes or until well browned.

- Turn the chicken thighs and cook for a further 2 minutes on the other side or until well browned. Reduce the heat to low, add the stock, cover loosely with a lid and simmer for 7–8 minutes or until the chicken is just cooked through (the juices will run clear when pierced with a skewer or fork).

- Transfer the chicken thighs from the frying pan to a chopping board. Increase the heat to high and reduce the liquid in the pan. Meanwhile slice the chicken into small bite-sized pieces. When the liquid in the pan has reduced by half, return the chicken to the pan. Increase the heat to high and stir-fry for 2–3 minutes until the liquid is soaked up and the chicken begins to char.

- Meanwhile toast the soft corn tortillas in a dry pan set over a medium-high heat for around 30–40 seconds on each side. As the tortillas are toasted, wrap them in a clean tea towel or place in a tortilla basket to keep warm.

- Arrange the tortillas in twos on a serving plate. Spread a little sour cream on each one, top with the taco beef, Pico de Gallo and Salsa Verde and serve.

FISH TACOS WITH RED CABBAGE SLAW

Serves 2

Often made using mahi mahi, fish tacos are light and healthy but oh-so delicious! Mahi mahi is found in tropical or sub-tropical waters and is commonly used for tacos. Any firm white fish such as cod or haddock will also work well. For added crunch, serve with a handful of tortilla chips.

½ teaspoon garlic powder
¼ teaspoon cumin powder
¼ teaspoon paprika
Pinch of cayenne pepper
Pinch of sea salt and black pepper
1 tablespoon lime juice
1 tablespoon vegetable oil
300g cod (or other white fish, around 2–3 fillets)
12 small soft corn tortillas (6 per person)
Sour cream, Pico de Gallo and Salsa Verde (pages 205 and
    200), to serve

Slaw
½ red cabbage, finely sliced
1 small red onion, peeled, halved and finely sliced
Handful of fresh coriander leaves, finely chopped
1 tablespoon lime juice
1 teaspoon olive oil

Pinch of sea salt
Pinch of black pepper

- In a bowl, place the garlic powder, cumin powder, paprika, cayenne pepper, sea salt, black pepper, lime juice and vegetable oil. Mix well.

- Arrange the fish on a baking tray. Top with the prepared spices and mix well until all of the fish is coated. Set aside for 5 minutes.

- Preheat the oven to 200°C/Gas 6. Meanwhile make the Slaw: add sliced red cabbage, red onion, coriander leaves, lime juice, olive oil, sea salt and black pepper to a bowl. Mix well and set aside whilst the fish cooks. Alternatively, prepare in advance, cover and chill in the refrigerator for up to 24 hours ahead of cooking.

- Bake the fish for around 12–15 minutes or until flaky and cooked through.

- Toast the soft corn tortillas in a dry pan set over a medium-high heat for around 30–40 seconds on each side. As the tortillas are toasted, wrap them in a clean tea towel or place in a tortilla basket to keep warm.

- Remove the fish from the oven and break into small–medium pieces with a fork.

- Arrange the tortillas in twos on a warmed serving plate. Spread a little sour cream on each one, top with the spiced fish, prepared Slaw, Pico de Gallo and Salsa Verde.

CHICKEN FRANKIE (INDIAN
SPICED CHICKEN WRAP)

Serves 1

Also known as 'katia roll', this Mumbai-style wrap or 'Frankie' combines spicy, flavoursome chicken with crisp, oily paratha-style bread for the ultimate sandwich, finished with fresh salad leaves and tomatoes. Chapati flour is available in the larger supermarkets and from Indian grocers.

  1 skinless, boneless chicken breast fillet (around 113g weight)
  ½ teaspoon Garlic & Ginger Paste (page 228)
  Pinch of cumin powder
  Pinch of garam masala
  ½ teaspoon dried fenugreek leaves (also known as 'methi')
  ¼ teaspoon paprika
  ¼ teaspoon chilli powder
  Pinch of sea salt
  ½ teaspoon distilled white vinegar
  1 teaspoon vegetable oil, plus extra for deep-frying
  2 teaspoons potato flour or cornflour
  1 teaspoon lemon juice
  Coriander Chutney (page 235), sliced salad tomatoes, sliced red onions and finely chopped fresh coriander, to serve

Paratha-style wrap ('Frankie')

125g chapati flour, plus extra for rolling out

Pinch of baking powder

Pinch of sea salt

1 tablespoon natural yogurt

Around 60ml water

1–2 tablespoons vegetable oil, plus extra for brushing

1 egg, whisked

- Trim any excess fat from the chicken breast and cut into 5–6 pieces. Place the chicken in a food-safe bowl and add the Garlic & Ginger Paste, cumin powder, garam masala, dried fenugreek leaves, paprika, chilli powder, sea salt, vinegar and vegetable oil. Mix well. Add the potato flour or cornflour, mix well once again, cover and place in the refrigerator for 1–2 hours.

- Prepare the Frankie wraps: In a bowl, place the chapati flour, baking powder and sea salt. Mix well. Add the yogurt and water and mix well once again until the dough comes together. Empty the dough onto a floured surface. Knead for 2–3 minutes or until smooth. Return the dough to the bowl, cover with a clean damp cloth and set aside to rest for 30 minutes.

- Divide the dough into two pieces. Roll each piece of dough into a ball. On a floured surface, carefully roll one of the dough balls out into a 15–20cm circle. Brush the rolled-out dough with a little vegetable oil. Roll the dough up like a sausage and, using floured hands, form into a dough ball once again and roll out again into a 20cm circle. This creates a layer of fat within the dough similar to that made when preparing pastry. The second dough ball can be frozen for future use.

- Heat a tava (see Box page 82) or large frying pan over a medium-high heat until just beginning to smoke. Lower the heat to medium-low and place the rolled-out bread in the pan. Cook the bread for around 1 minute, turning every 10–15 seconds. Brush one side of the bread with some of the beaten egg. Continue cooking for a further 2 minutes, brushing with a little oil and flipping the bread every 10–15 seconds. When the bread is crisp and charred, remove from the pan and cover with foil to soften. Set aside until needed.

- Heat the oil for deep-frying to around 180°C/356°F. Carefully place the marinated chicken pieces in the hot oil and fry for 3–4 minutes or until the chicken is fully cooked and crisp at the edges. Turn the pieces often as they cook. Remove the cooked chicken pieces from the pan, drain any excess oil and arrange on a plate. Add lemon juice and mix well. Slice the chicken into small pieces.

- To serve, spread 1 tablespoon Coriander Chutney onto the egg-topped side of the bread. Add the cooked chicken pieces and top with sliced tomatoes, red onions and fresh coriander. Roll the wrap up and serve with extra chutney on the side.

Tava

A tava pan is a large flat metal pan designed specifically for cooking flatbreads such as tortillas, chapattis and roti. The metal pan gets very hot and ensures the breads brown nicely and puff up when cooking.

HOG ROAST ROLLS WITH APPLE CHUTNEY

Serves 8

On Edinburgh's streets you can find more than one location selling these delicious rolls, piled high with roasted meats and served with chutneys and haggis. If desired, the apple chutney may be made in advance or in larger quantities, ladled into sterilised jars and stored at room temperature for up to three months.

½ teaspoon Chinese five-spice
½ teaspoon dried mixed herbs
½ teaspoon sea salt
¼ teaspoon black pepper
2.5kg rolled and tied pork shoulder
1 tablespoon vegetable oil
Soft white rolls and butter, to serve

Apple Chutney
1 tablespoon vegetable oil
2 onions, peeled and finely chopped
1 large red chilli pepper, deseeded and finely chopped
  (see also page 33)
1 large garlic clove, peeled and crushed
4 apples, finely chopped (no need to peel)
60ml apple cider vinegar
2 tablespoons caster sugar

2 tablespoons soft brown sugar
Pinch of dried mixed herbs
2–3 tablespoons water

- For the chutney, heat the vegetable oil in a saucepan set over a medium heat. Add the onions and chilli. Cook for 5–6 minutes, stirring often. Add the garlic and apples and cook for a further 2 minutes.

- Add the cider vinegar, caster sugar, brown sugar, mixed herbs and water. Mix well, almost fully cover and cook on a medium-low heat, stirring occasionally, for around 15 minutes or until the apples have softened and no liquid remains. Once cooked, set aside to cool. The chutney can be stored in the refrigerator for 3–4 days; however, remove it from the refrigerator about an hour before use to bring to room temperature.

- For the pork, preheat the oven to 220°C/Gas 7. In a small bowl, combine the Chinese five-spice, mixed herbs, sea salt and black pepper. Score the pork fat with a sharp knife and arrange the pork shoulder in a roasting tray. Rub the spice mix all over the pork and set aside for 5 minutes.

- Rub the vegetable oil all around the seasoned pork. Place into the oven, cook for 30 minutes and then remove and cover tightly with foil. Reduce the heat to 120°C/Gas ½ and return the pork to the oven. Cook for 5 hours.

- Remove the pork from the oven and remove the foil, reserving it for use later. Increase the temperature to

220°C/Gas 7 and return the pork to the oven for a further 30 minutes. Remove, cover with the reserved foil and allow to rest at room temperature for 20 minutes. If desired, the fat may be cut from the pork and returned to the hot oven on its own for a further few minutes for extra-crispy crackling.

• Shred or pull the pork using two forks or clean hands. Pile the pork generously on top of well-buttered bread rolls and serve with the prepared chutney.

NYC PIZZA SLICE

Makes 1 large or 2 medium pizzas

Thin, crisp and chewy crusts with sweet tomato sauce and stretchy, oily mozzarella, New York City pizza slices are the perfect street food. Ordered by the slice, usually for only around $2, there's no reason not to have another.

NYC-style pizza crusts have a unique, well-developed flavour. Many attribute this to the Big Apple's water, with some pizza sellers in various states across America even going to the lengths of importing water directly from New York. In truth, the depth of flavour more likely comes from the cold and slow, two- to three-day rise the dough is given before use. This natural process results in a crust full of natural flavour.

¾ teaspoon sea salt
½ teaspoon sugar
¼ teaspoon fast-action dried yeast
200g strong white bread flour, plus extra for rolling out
125ml water (imported from New York, if you so desire!)
1 teaspoon virgin olive oil, plus extra for oiling the dough
75g mozzarella (I use pre-packaged and pre-grated)
Dried oregano and black pepper, to serve

Sauce
100ml passata
1 teaspoon olive oil

¼ teaspoon sea salt
½ teaspoon sugar
¼ teaspoon dried Italian herbs
Pinch of garlic powder
Pinch of onion powder

- In a large bowl, place the sea salt, sugar and dried yeast. Mix well. Add the bread flour and mix well once again. Add the water and olive oil and mix well until a dough is formed.

- Empty the dough onto a well-floured board and knead for 3–4 minutes until smooth. Slightly oil the dough ball, place in a food-safe container or bag (allowing room for the dough to expand) and set aside in the refrigerator. The dough may be used after just a few hours, but for a NYC-style crust, ideally allow it to prove in the refrigerator for two days.

- Make the sauce: In a bowl, place the passata, olive oil, sea salt, sugar, dried Italian herbs, garlic powder and onion powder. Mix well and set aside until needed.

- Heat a pizza stone (see page 88) in the oven at the highest possible heat for at least 1 hour. Remove the dough from the refrigerator 20 minutes before cooking. Dust the work surface with flour and pat the dough out into a round. Press down with your fingertips, stretching and working it to form a large thin pizza dough. Avoid using a rolling pin as this will knock the air out of the dough.

- Arrange the prepared pizza base on a well-floured board. Top the pizza with 2–3 tablespoons of sauce. Add mozzarella cheese. Top the mozzarella with a few more drops of pizza sauce.

- Slide the prepared pizza directly onto the hot pizza stone. Bake for around 6 minutes or until the cheese has melted and the crust is golden brown and crisp. Remove the pizza from the oven and top with dried oregano and black pepper.

- The pizza can be served immediately; however, NYC pizzas are also often reheated to order by the slice. To reheat a slice, heat a dry frying pan over a high heat. Place the pizza slice in the frying pan, cover with a lid and reduce the heat to medium. Cook untouched for 3 minutes. Lift up the lid and drop around 1 teaspoon water into the pan beside the pizza. Immediately replace the lid and allow the steam to heat the top of the pizza. The reheated pizza should have a golden crust underneath and soft, melted cheese on top.

Pizza Stones

For an authentic crust and best results, it's worth investing in a pizza stone. Preheated in the oven for up to 1 hour, pizza stones lock in heat and ensure that the crust is golden, crispy and cooked through. If you don't have one, a good-quality baking tray preheated until very hot provides a good alternative.

ZAPIEKANKA (POLISH PIZZA)

Serves 2

Take your French bread pizza to new levels by adding a savoury, umami element from cooked onions and mushrooms. For a snack prepared so quickly, this is a delicious treat. Don't be tempted to leave out the ketchup – it combines with the other ingredients to create a unique flavour!

1 tablespoon vegetable oil
1 tablespoon butter
10–12 white button mushrooms, finely chopped
1 onion, peeled and finely chopped
1 large baguette
100g grated Cheddar cheese
100g grated mozzarella cheese (I use pre-packaged and pre-grated but sliced fresh mozzarella also offers good results)
Pinch of sea salt
Pinch of black pepper
Pinch of dried oregano
Tomato ketchup, to serve

- Heat the oil and butter in a frying pan set over a medium-high heat. Add the chopped mushrooms and onion and mix well. Stir-fry for 2–3 minutes. Reduce the heat to medium and continue cooking for a further 5–6 minutes or until all the liquid has cooked off and the mushrooms and onions are sautéed. Transfer to a bowl and set aside to cool briefly.

- Preheat the oven to 200°C/Gas 6. Meanwhile slice the baguette in half and slice each half down the middle to create 4 bread slices. Arrange the bread slices on a baking tray. Spoon the mushroom and onion mixture onto each bread slice. Top with Cheddar and mozzarella. Place the baking tray in the oven for around 10–15 minutes or until the bread is crispy and the cheese is golden and bubbling.

- Remove the Zapiekanka from the oven and garnish with sea salt, black pepper and dried oregano. Add a generous amount of ketchup and serve.

LANGOS (HUNGARIAN FRIED BREAD)

Serves 2

Probably the best garlic bread you'll ever make, this deep-fried flatbread is light, crispy and impossible to resist. The fried langos bread can also be topped with mozzarella cheese and finished briefly under the grill for a delicious fried pizza variation.

Pinch of sugar
Pinch of sea salt
½ teaspoon fast-action dried yeast
100g plain flour, plus extra for rolling out
Around 60ml water
Vegetable oil for proving and deep-frying

Garlic Butter
1 tablespoon salted butter, softened
½ teaspoon garlic powder
Pinch of dried parsley
Pinch of sea salt
Pinch of black pepper

• Make the garlic butter: In a bowl, place the softened salted butter, garlic powder, dried parsley, sea salt and black pepper. Mix well and set aside.

- In a large bowl, place the sugar, sea salt and yeast; mix well. Add the plain flour and mix well again. Add the water and mix until a dough forms.

- Empty the dough out onto a well-floured board and knead for 3–4 minutes or until smooth, adding more flour as necessary. Lightly oil another bowl, place the dough inside, cover with a clean damp cloth and set aside for around 1 hour to prove.

- Heat the oil to around 180°C/356°F. Divide the dough in half and press out into rounds of medium thickness. Carefully place one Langos bread in the hot oil and deep-fry for around 2–3 minutes, turning once during cooking.

- Once cooked, drain any excess oil from the Langos breads and arrange on a serving plate. Top generously with the garlic butter and serve.

SOCCA (FARINATA) CHICKPEA BREAD

Makes 2 breads (enough to serve 4)

Made using gram (chickpea) flour, this bread is deliciously light. It is designed to be eaten out of paper on the street but would also be delicious topped with roasted red peppers or a fresh Street Salad (page 46).

100g gram (chickpea) flour
1 teaspoon sea salt
½ teaspoon black pepper
Pinch of white pepper
Pinch of garlic powder
Pinch of paprika
240ml water
2 tablespoons virgin olive oil, plus extra for cooking
1 onion, peeled and finely sliced

- In a blender, place the gram (chickpea) flour, sea salt, black pepper, white pepper, garlic powder, paprika, water and olive oil. Blend thoroughly, cover and set the mixture aside overnight at room temperature (the batter may be left in the blender bowl or transferred to a food-safe bowl).

- Heat a touch of oil in a frying pan and stir-fry the sliced onions for 5–6 minutes or until golden and slightly crisp.

Allow to cool slightly, add to the prepared chickpea batter and mix thoroughly.

- Preheat the oven to around 220°C/Gas 7. Meanwhile lightly grease two medium-large baking tins*. Pour the batter mix into each tin, creating a thin layer. Don't pour too much batter into each tin or the resulting bread will be a little too thick.

- Bake the Socca in the centre of the oven for around 12–14 minutes or until golden and cooked through. Remove from the oven and brush with a little extra oil or Garlic Butter (page 91).

- Preheat the grill to medium-high. Place the Socca breads under the grill and toast for 1–2 minutes until sizzling and golden. Set aside to cool for 1–2 minutes, then slice and serve warm.

    * I use 30cm/12in baking tins but any baking tin will produce good results. The key is to cook the Socca in thin layers to ensure it cooks through. If using a smaller tin, simply cook the bread in several smaller batches.

BANH MHI (VIETNAMESE SANDWICH)

Serves 1

Banh Mhi translates as 'bread wheat' and is used to describe
all kinds of bread. This sandwich uses a light, crispy baguette
introduced to Vietnam by the French but a traditional French-
style baguette will also produce good results.

1 French baguette
1 tablespoon mayonnaise
2 teaspoons hoisin sauce
Handful of fresh coriander leaves, finely chopped
1 fresh chilli pepper, deseeded and finely sliced (optional)
  (see also page 33)
1 teaspoon sriracha sauce (from supermarkets)

Pork Filling
½ teaspoon light soy sauce
½ teaspoon dark soy sauce
1 teaspoon oyster sauce
Dash of fish sauce
½ teaspoon soft brown sugar
1 teaspoon rice wine
1 teaspoon lime juice
1 tablespoon vegetable oil
¼ teaspoon potato flour or cornflour
Pinch of white pepper
225g pork loin fillet, thinly sliced

Pickled Vegetables
1 small carrot, peeled and grated
½ cucumber, thinly sliced
2–3 red radishes, trimmed and thinly sliced
1 tablespoon caster sugar
1 tablespoon rice wine vinegar
Pinch of sea salt

- In a bowl, place the soy sauces, oyster sauce, fish sauce, rice wine, lime juice, vegetable oil, white pepper and potato flour or cornflour. Mix well to combine. Add the pork slices and mix thoroughly. Cover and set aside in the refrigerator for 30 minutes.

- In another bowl, mix together the Pickled Vegetables ingredients. Cover and set aside for 30 minutes.

- Heat a wok or large frying pan over a high heat. Add the pork slices, discarding any leftover marinade. Stir-fry over a high heat for 3–4 minutes or until the pork is slightly charred and cooked through. Remove and set aside.

- Slice the baguette down the middle. Spread one side of the bread with mayonnaise and the other with hoisin sauce. Arrange the cooked pork over one side of the bread. Top with fresh coriander leaves and fresh chillies. Drizzle with as much sriracha sauce as you desire and serve.

BREAKFAST BANH MHI (VIETNAMESE PORK & FRIED EGG BAGUETTE)

Serves 1

Spicy and comforting, this sandwich is the perfect morning after pick-me-up! Shaoxing rice wine is widely available in larger supermarkets. A dry sherry provides similar results.

1 teaspoon, plus 100ml vegetable oil

100g pork mince

¼ teaspoon Garlic & Ginger Paste (page 228)

1 teaspoon Shaoxing rice wine

1 teaspoon hoisin sauce

Dash of dark soy sauce

Pinch of Chinese five-spice

Pinch of ground Sichuan peppercorns (optional, but recommended)

50ml water

1 egg

½ large baguette

1 tablespoon mayonnaise

1 tablespoon sriracha sauce (from supermarkets)

1 red Thai chilli, deseeded and finely sliced (see also page 33), fresh coriander and mint leaves, finely chopped, to garnish

- Heat 1 teaspoon of oil in a wok or large frying pan set over a high heat. Add the pork mince and stir-fry for 30–40 seconds until broken up and beginning to brown. Lower the heat to medium and add the Garlic & Ginger Paste and rice wine. Mix well.

- Add the hoisin sauce, dark soy sauce, Chinese five-spice, Sichuan peppercorns (if using) and water. Mix well and simmer for 8–10 minutes. As the liquid reduces and the pork is nearly cooked, increase the heat to high and allow it to catch a little on the pan. Those crispy pork bits are the best part!

- Add 100ml of oil to the pan over a medium heat. Fry the egg, carefully spooning hot oil over the top of the yolk. Cooking the egg in this way is very traditional in crispy edges and a soft yolk.

- Slice the baguette in half and spread mayonnaise on one half and sriracha sauce on the other. Spoon the cooked pork mince onto the baguette and top with the crispy fried egg. Garnish with chilli, fresh coriander and fresh mint. Serve with extra sriracha sauce on the side.

CHEESESTEAK

Serves 1

Made famous in Philadelphia, a well-made cheesesteak sand-wich is a thing of beauty and simplicity. Thin shavings of steak, flash-fried alongside onion, garlic and pepper, covered in melted cheese and scooped up inside a bread roll. What's not to love?

1 rib-eye steak (around 225g weight)
2 teaspoons vegetable oil
1 small onion, peeled and finely sliced
½ green pepper, deseeded and finely sliced
1 garlic clove, peeled and crushed
Pinch of dried oregano
¼ teaspoon sea salt
¼ teaspoon black pepper
1 large French baguette or similar
1–2 slices of Emmental cheese or processed cheese slices

- Cut the rib-eye steak into very small, thin slices. Add 1 teaspoon of vegetable oil, mix well and set aside.

- Heat the remaining teaspoon of vegetable oil in a wok or large frying pan set over a medium-high heat. Add the sliced onion and green pepper. Stir-fry for 3–4 minutes. Add the crushed garlic and dried oregano and season with salt and pepper. Mix well once more and push the cooked vegetables to one corner of the pan.

- Increase the heat to high. Add the steak slices and stir-fry for 2–3 minutes or until browned and just cooked. Stir the cooked vegetables through the steak and stir-fry for a further 30 seconds.

- Preheat the grill to high. Slice the baguette down the middle and arrange on a baking tray. Spoon the steak and vegetables onto the bread and arrange the cheese slices on top. Place under the grill for 1–2 minutes or until the bread is warm and the cheese has melted. Slice the sandwich in half and serve.

DISCO FRY EGG

Serves 1

Quick, easy and utterly delicious, this spicy bread omelette is the perfect energy booster.

2 teaspoons vegetable oil
½ onion, peeled and finely chopped
1–2 finger chillies, deseeded and finely sliced (see also page 33)
Handful of fresh coriander leaves, finely chopped
1 egg
2 pinches of sea salt
2 pinches of turmeric
2 pinches of garam masala
2 pinches of chilli powder
1 soft white bread roll, sliced open

- Heat 1 teaspoon of oil in a frying pan set over a medium heat. Add half of the chopped onion, chillies and fresh coriander leaves. Allow to cook for a few seconds.

- Crack the egg into the pan on top of the onions etc. Immediately burst the yolk and spread the mix around a little. Add 1 pinch each of sea salt, turmeric, garam masala and chilli powder. Slice open the bread roll and press it down onto the cooking spiced egg mixture. Top with the remaining sea salt, turmeric, garam masala and chilli powder and another teaspoon of oil.

- Use a spatula to press the bread roll down hard into the cooking egg mixture. After around 30 seconds, the bread and egg should set together. Flip the bread/egg and press down hard again with the spatula. Continue to cook and flip the bread omelette for 1–2 minutes or until cooked and crispy.

- Arrange the Disco Fry Egg on a warmed serving plate and serve with the remaining raw chopped onion, sliced chillies and fresh coriander leaves.

GRILLED SANDWICHES

Serves 1

More commonly known as a 'toastie' in the UK, grilled cheese trucks are a big part of the American street food scene, with many offering a wide variety of fantastical and fun fillings. Although sandwich grills have their nostalgic place, it's worth learning to cook your grilled cheese sandwiches in a frying pan. The method for a classic grilled cheese sandwich below will get you started, along with a filling suggestion you might like to experiment with!

2 slices white bread
2 teaspoons salted butter
30g grated Cheddar cheese
15g grated mozzarella cheese
Pinch of sea salt
Pinch of black pepper
Pinch of white pepper

- Butter both slices of bread and arrange them on top of each other, buttered sides meeting (like a sandwich with no filling). Arrange the grated Cheddar and mozzarella cheeses on the top slice of bread. Sprinkle with sea salt, black and white pepper.

- Preheat a dry frying pan over a medium heat. Lift the cheese-topped bread slice and place carefully inside the frying pan, butter side down. Place the remaining bread slice on top, butter side up.

- Cook the grilled sandwich on one side for around 3 minutes or until golden and toasted. Carefully turn the sandwich and cook for a further 3 minutes or until golden and toasted on both sides. The melting cheese will hold things together; there should be no need to apply any pressure to the sandwich.

- Once cooked, arrange the sandwich on a warmed serving plate and slice diagonally to form two triangles. Press down gently in the middle of each and push the two halves together again; this will push a little of the melted cheese out and is a trick used to ensure a stringy, stretchy result when the customer lifts the sandwich for their first bite.

For a spicy variation, try adding 1 teaspoon sriracha sauce and half a thinly sliced apple.

4

FRYING TONIGHT

During the Second World War, chip shops in the UK suffered, as did everyone, from rationing and irregular supplies. Locals soon knew to look out for the 'Frying Tonight' sign in shop windows, an indication that the proprietor had stock and would be open for business that evening.

Fried foods have received a lot of criticism over the years, some warranted and some not so. Recent studies suggest that a diet rich in healthy fats can in fact be beneficial to health, contrary to previously promoted expert opinion. Using good fats and oils for frying (coconut oil is amongst the latest of popular choices) and ensuring that food is cooked at the right temperature, fried food can certainly hold its place as part of a healthy diet.

As fried food is cooked at such a high temperature, the cooking process is usually very quick, perhaps 5–6 minutes for most recipes. This makes it ideal for street food vendors (and us!) as it allows prior preparation to be completed and a simple task of frying up portions at a time of our chosen recipe as and when hungry customers or guests are ready to eat.

If you're serious about recipes that involve deep-frying, there are various modern-day fryers around which will do a great job of making sure the fat reaches the correct temperature and is filtered and cleaned after use etc. Whilst these are certainly worth considering, a wok or large frying pan filled a third full with fat will be absolutely fine too. If you do decide to go with a wok or frying pan, however, a frying thermometer is highly recommended in order to ensure your food is frying at the right temperature. Getting this right is the key to crispy results.

Some Safety Advice

When cooking with hot oil, remember never to leave the pan unattended. Ensure handles are turned the right way to avoid spillages – and be careful! After cooking, allow the oil to cool completely before attempting to move the pan.

TAIWANESE FRIED CHICKEN

Serves 1

Salty, spicy, sweet ... These fried chicken escalopes are impossible to resist!

1 teaspoon sea salt
½ teaspoon ground Sichuan pepper
¼ teaspoon black pepper
Pinch of white pepper
¼ teaspoon Chinese five-spice
Pinch of sugar
1 skinless, boneless chicken breast fillet (around 113g weight)
1 teaspoon rice wine
Dash of toasted sesame oil
½ teaspoon light soy sauce
1 egg
5–6 tablespoons potato flour or cornflour
Vegetable oil for deep-frying
Sweet & Sour Dipping Sauce (page 225), to serve

- In a bowl, place the sea salt, Sichuan pepper, black pepper, white pepper, Chinese five-spice and sugar. Mix well and set aside.

- Trim any excess fat from the chicken breast fillet. Arrange the chicken breast on top of a piece of food-safe wrap or greaseproof paper. Cover with more wrap or paper and use a meat mallet to pound the chicken breast into a large flat escalope. Add the rice wine, toasted sesame oil, light soy sauce and a pinch of the prepared spicy salt. Mix well and set aside for 5 minutes.

- Beat the egg thoroughly in a separate bowl. Add the potato flour or cornflour to another bowl. Dip the chicken breast in the beaten egg. Drain off any excess and place the chicken breast in the bowl of potato flour or cornflour, patting the meat down into the flour until well coated.

- Heat oil for deep-frying to around 180°C/356°F. Fry the breaded chicken slice for 4–5 minutes or until cooked through, golden and crisp. Remove, drain off any excess oil and set aside to rest on kitchen paper for 1 minute.

- Slice the fried chicken into 4–5 pieces and arrange on a warmed serving plate. Season with roughly ¼ teaspoon of the spicy salt mix and serve with Sweet & Sour Dipping Sauce on the side.

CHICKEN 65 (INDIAN FRIED CHICKEN)

Serves 1

From Hyderabad, this spicy chicken is the perfect snack or can be added to curry sauces and even tacos. Fans of chicken tikka will quickly come to love this dish.

1 skinless, boneless chicken breast fillet (around 113g)
½ teaspoon Garlic & Ginger Paste (page 228)
¼ teaspoon paprika
¼ teaspoon chilli powder
Pinch of cumin powder
Pinch of garam masala
½ teaspoon dried fenugreek leaves (also known as methi)
Pinch of sea salt
½ teaspoon distilled white vinegar
1 teaspoon vegetable oil, plus extra for deep-frying
Handful of fresh coriander leaves, finely chopped, to garnish
Finely sliced onion and lemon wedges, to serve

- Trim any excess fat from the chicken breast and cut into 5–6 bite-sized pieces. Place in a bowl and add the Garlic & Ginger Paste, paprika, chilli powder, cumin powder, garam masala, dried fenugreek leaves, sea salt, distilled white vinegar and a teaspoon of vegetable oil. Mix thoroughly, cover and set aside in the refrigerator to marinate for 1–2 hours.

- Heat the oil for deep-frying to around 180°C/356°F. Carefully place the chicken pieces in the hot oil and fry for 4–5 minutes or until cooked through and golden. Remove from the pan and drain off any excess oil on kitchen paper. Arrange on a warmed serving plate, garnish with fresh coriander leaves and serve with finely sliced onion and lemon wedges.

BONELESS BUTTERMILK FRIED CHICKEN

Serves 2

Sometimes only fried chicken will do. Marinated overnight, the chicken will stay juicy and tender inside after frying. The seasoned coating on the outside turns a beautiful golden brown and the resulting chicken is deliciously addictive.

120ml buttermilk (or 120ml milk mixed with 1 teaspoon
   of distilled white vinegar and allowed to stand for 3–4
   minutes)
4–6 skinless, boneless chicken thigh fillets (450g)
180g plain flour
1 teaspoon sea salt
½ teaspoon white pepper
¼ teaspoon black pepper
½ teaspoon garlic powder
¼ teaspoon onion powder
1 teaspoon paprika
½ teaspoon cayenne pepper
½ teaspoon Italian dried herbs
¼ teaspoon dried sage
¼ teaspoon celery seeds
Vegetable oil for deep-frying
Coleslaw and BBQ Sauce (pages 218 and 38), to serve

- In a food-safe container, place the buttermilk and chicken thighs. Cover with a lid and refrigerate for at least 4 hours or, ideally, overnight.

- To a large bowl, add plain flour, sea salt, white pepper, black pepper, garlic powder, onion powder, paprika, cayenne pepper, Italian dried herbs, dried sage and celery seeds. Mix well.

- Keeping one hand dry, lift the chicken thigh fillets out of the buttermilk, allowing any excess to drain off. Press the chicken thighs into the flour mixture to coat well on all sides. Arrange the chicken on a plate and repeat until all of the chicken is ready to fry.

- Heat the oil to around 180°C/356°F. Carefully place the chicken thighs in the hot oil (fry in batches, if necessary). Fry for around 7–8 minutes or until golden brown and cooked through, turning just once during cooking.

- Remove the chicken from the pan and drain off any excess oil onto kitchen paper. Arrange on a warmed serving plate and serve with Coleslaw and a side of BBQ Sauce.

CHICKEN PARMO

Serves 2

Made famous in Middlesbrough in the UK, Chicken Parmo is fast becoming a street food regular at pop-ups and festivals.

50g Panko breadcrumbs
¼ teaspoon garlic powder
¼ teaspoon paprika
¼ teaspoon dried Italian herbs
Pinch of sea salt
Pinch of black pepper
1 egg, 50ml milk
3–4 tablespoons plain flour, seasoned with a pinch of sea salt and black pepper
2 skinless, boneless chicken breast fillets (around 113g each)
200ml of vegetable oil for deep-frying
2 handfuls of grated mozzarella° and French fries, to serve

Cheese Sauce
1 tablespoon salted butter
1 tablespoon plain flour
200ml milk
Pinch of nutmeg
75g grated Cheddar cheese

1 teaspoon yellow (American) mustard
¼ teaspoon sea salt
Pinch of black pepper

- Heat the butter in a saucepan set over a low heat. When the butter has melted, add the plain flour and cook for 1–2 minutes or until golden. Slowly add the milk, whisking thoroughly until the sauce becomes smooth. Add the nutmeg, grated Cheddar, yellow mustard, sea salt and black pepper. Mix well and simmer for 1–2 minutes or until the cheese has melted and the sauce is thick and smooth.

- In a bowl, place the Panko breadcrumbs, garlic powder, paprika, dried Italian herbs, sea salt and black pepper. Mix well and set aside.

- Whisk the egg and milk together in a separate bowl, and tip the seasoned flour onto a plate.

- Trim any excess fat from the chicken breast fillets. Arrange the chicken breasts on top of a piece of food-safe wrap or greaseproof paper. Cover with more wrap or paper and use a meat mallet to pound into large flat escalopes.

- Keeping one hand dry, dip each flattened chicken breast first into the seasoned flour, then into the egg and milk mixture and finally into the seasoned Panko breadcrumbs to coat. Transfer the breaded chicken to a plate.

- Heat the oil to around 180°C/356°F. Carefully place the breaded chicken in the hot oil. Fry for around 5–6 minutes or until golden brown and cooked through, turning just once during cooking. Meanwhile heat the grill to high. Remove the cooked chicken from the pan, drain off any excess oil onto kitchen paper and arrange on a baking tray.

- Top each chicken breast with a generous amount of cheese sauce and cover with mozzarella. Place the Chicken Parmos under the grill for 3–4 minutes or until the cheese is golden and melted. Serve with French fries.

  ° I use pre-purchased and pre-grated mozzarella from supermarkets. Fresh mozzarella, torn, would also provide good results.

HAND-BREADED CHICKEN TENDERS

Serves 2

The combination of crispy Panko breadcrumbs and sesame seeds makes these Tenders extra-crunchy. For a spicy variation, add a little hot sauce to the beaten egg before breading the chicken pieces.

1 tablespoon sesame seeds
80g Panko breadcrumbs
2 tablespoons potato flour or cornflour
½ teaspoon garlic powder
¼ teaspoon onion powder
¼ teaspoon cayenne pepper
½ teaspoon dried Italian herbs
½ teaspoon sea salt
Pinch of black pepper
Pinch of white pepper
1 egg
50ml milk
3–4 tablespoons plain flour, seasoned with a pinch of sea salt and black pepper
2 skinless, boneless chicken breast fillets (around 113g each)
Vegetable oil for deep-frying
3 tablespoons BBQ Sauce (page 38), plus extra to serve
Handful of mixed salad leaves, to serve

- Toast the sesame seeds in a dry frying pan set over a medium heat for 2–3 minutes or until golden. Set aside.

- To a bowl, add Panko breadcrumbs, potato flour or corn-flour, garlic powder, onion powder, cayenne pepper, dried Italian herbs, sea salt, black and white pepper. Mix well.

- Whisk the egg and milk in a separate bowl and transfer the seasoned flour to a plate.

- Trim any excess fat from the chicken breast fillets and cut each one into 5–6 long thin strips. Keeping one hand dry, dip the chicken strips first in the seasoned flour, then into the egg and milk mixture and finally into the seasoned Panko breadcrumbs to coat. Arrange the breaded strips on a plate and repeat until all of the chicken is breaded and ready to fry.

- Heat the oil to around 180°C/356°F. Carefully place the breaded chicken strips in the hot oil. Fry for around 5–6 minutes or until golden brown and cooked through, turning occasionally. Remove from the pan and drain off any excess oil onto kitchen paper. Coat the fried chicken generously with BBQ Sauce.

- Arrange the salad leaves on a serving plate. Place the Chicken Tenders on top, sprinkle with toasted sesame seeds and serve with extra BBQ Sauce on the side.

DAKGANGJEONG (KOREAN CANDIED FRIED CHICKEN)

Serves 2

Crispy, crunchy and sweet, this chicken is delicious when hot and doesn't lose its crunch when cold. Boneless chicken thighs offer the taste and succulence of wings without the distraction of bones!

4–6 skinless, boneless chicken thigh fillets (around 450g total weight)
Pinch of sea salt
Pinch of black pepper
1 teaspoon rice wine
Vegetable oil for deep-frying
2 spring onions, trimmed, peeled and finely sliced, and toasted sesame seeds, to serve

Sauce
1 teaspoon vegetable oil
1 teaspoon Garlic & Ginger Paste (page 228)
1 teaspoon dried chilli flakes
1 teaspoon light soy sauce
1 teaspoon dark soy sauce
1 tablespoon rice wine vinegar
2 tablespoons soft brown sugar
1 tablespoon clear honey

Pinch of white pepper
Dash of sesame oil
2–3 tablespoons water

Batter
60g self-raising flour
90g potato flour or cornflour
¼ teaspoon sea salt
½ teaspoon black pepper
1½ teaspoons sugar
175ml water

- To make the sauce, place the vegetable oil, Garlic & Ginger Paste, dried chilli flakes, soy sauces, rice wine vinegar, brown sugar, honey, white pepper, sesame oil and water in a saucepan. Mix well to combine and set aside.

- For the batter, add self-raising flour, potato flour or corn-flour, sea salt, black pepper, sugar and water to a bowl. Whisk thoroughly until smooth and set aside.

- Trim any excess fat from the chicken thighs and cut each thigh into 4 pieces. Place the chicken pieces in a food-safe bowl and add salt, black pepper and rice wine. Set aside.

- Heat the oil for deep-frying to around 170°C/338°F. Dip each chicken piece in the batter mix then carefully place in the hot oil. Fry the chicken pieces in batches for around 3–4 minutes or until just cooked through and a little golden.

- Remove from the pan and drain off any excess oil on kitchen paper. Increase the heat of the oil to around 190°C/374°F. Return the chicken pieces to the pan and fry once more for 1–2 minutes or until golden and crunchy. Remove from the pan and drain off any excess oil on kitchen paper.

- Heat the prepared sauce for 2–3 minutes over a high heat, stirring, until the sauce has thickened. Transfer the cooked fried chicken to a large warmed bowl, top with sauce and mix thoroughly until each chicken piece is coated evenly.

- Arrange the candied fried chicken on a warmed serving plate and top with spring onions and toasted sesame seeds to serve.

THAI CHICKEN BALLS

Serves 2

Light and aromatic, these chicken balls are an ideal starter or side dish with your favourite Thai stir-fry.

2 skinless, boneless chicken breast fillets (each around 113g weight), diced
Pinch of coriander powder
Dash of light soy sauce
1 tablespoon sweet chilli sauce
1 teaspoon lime juice
2 tablespoons Panko breadcrumbs
1 spring onion, trimmed, peeled and sliced
Handful of fresh coriander leaves, finely chopped (reserve a few leaves for the garnish)
Vegetable oil for deep-frying
Sweet & Sour Dipping Sauce (page 225), to serve

- To a blender bowl, add the diced chicken, coriander powder, light soy sauce, sweet chilli sauce, lime juice, breadcrumbs, spring onion and fresh coriander leaves. Pulse 7–8 times until the chicken is minced and has blended well with the other ingredients. Using oiled hands, form small meatballs from the mixture.

- Heat the oil for deep-frying to around 180°C/356°F. Carefully place the chicken balls in the hot oil and fry for 3–4 minutes or until golden and cooked through.

- Remove the chicken balls from the pan, drain off any excess oil onto kitchen paper and arrange on a warmed serving plate. Garnish with a little extra fresh coriander and serve with Sweet & Sour Dipping Sauce.

THAI PRAWN FRITTERS

Serves 2

Bite-sized fritters, a little crisp on the outside and full of flavour. Delicious.

400g raw king prawns
2 Thai chilli peppers, deseeded and roughly chopped (see also page 33)
1 egg white
1½ teaspoons Garlic & Ginger Paste (page 228)
½ teaspoon light soy sauce
1 teaspoon rice wine
Pinch of white pepper
Handful of fresh coriander leaves, plus extra to garnish
2–3 tablespoons potato flour or cornflour
Vegetable oil for deep-frying
Sweet Chilli Tamarind Sauce (page 148), to serve

- To a blender bowl add the king prawns, chilli peppers, egg white, Garlic & Ginger Paste, light soy sauce, rice wine, white pepper and fresh coriander leaves. Pulse 4–5 times until blended to a paste.

- Transfer the prawn mix to a food-safe bowl, add the potato flour or cornflour and mix well. Cover and set aside in the refrigerator for 1 hour.

- Heat the oil to around 180°C/356°F. Using two teaspoons, carefully drop small teaspoon-sized amounts into the hot oil. Fry the prawn fritters in batches for around 3–4 minutes or until golden on all sides, then remove from the pan and drain any excess oil onto kitchen paper.

- Arrange on a warmed serving plate. Garnish with a little extra fresh coriander and serve with Sweet Chilli Tamarind Sauce.

COCONUT KING PRAWNS

Serves 2

Adding coconut flour to the breading makes these king prawns deliciously sweet and fragrant. Coconut flour is widely available in the larger supermarkets. However, desiccated coconut will provide good results if it's all you can find.

50g Panko breadcrumbs
2 tablespoons coconut flour
Pinch of sea salt
Pinch of cayenne pepper
1 egg
2 tablespoons milk
400g raw king prawns
Vegetable oil for deep-frying
Sweet Chilli Tamarind Sauce and Thai Sticky Rice (pages 148 and 169), to serve

- To a bowl, add the Panko breadcrumbs, coconut flour, sea salt and cayenne pepper. Mix well.

- In another bowl, whisk the egg and milk thoroughly to combine.

- Keeping one hand dry, dip each king prawn first in the egg and milk mixture and then in the coconut breadcrumbs. Set each one aside on a plate until all of the prawns are thoroughly breaded.

- Heat the oil to around 180°C/356°F. Carefully place each breaded king prawn in the hot oil and fry for 3–4 minutes or until the prawns are cooked through and the coating is golden and crispy.

- Drain off any excess oil on kitchen paper and arrange the Coconut King Prawns on a warmed serving plate. Serve with sides of Sweet Chilli Tamarind Sauce and Thai Sticky Rice.

MAC 'N' CHEESE BITES

Serves 1–2

Though these bites are undoubtedly the ultimate way to use up leftovers, the truth is they're so good you'll whip up a batch of Mac 'n' Cheese solely with these in mind.

4 tablespoons plain flour, seasoned with a little sea salt and black pepper
1 egg
50ml semi-skimmed milk
6 tablespoons Panko breadcrumbs
¼ teaspoon garlic powder
¼ teaspoon onion powder
½ teaspoon dried Italian herbs
Pinch of cayenne pepper
Pinch of sea salt
Pinch of black pepper
5–6 tablespoons cooked, cooled and chilled Mac 'n' Cheese (page 25)
Vegetable oil for deep-frying

- Sprinkle the seasoned flour over a large plate.

- In a small bowl, combine the egg and semi-skimmed milk and whisk thoroughly.

- In a large bowl, combine the Panko breadcrumbs, garlic powder, onion powder, dried Italian herbs, cayenne pepper, sea salt and black pepper.

- With lightly floured hands, work with around 1 tablespoon of the Mac 'n' cheese at a time. Keeping one hand dry, dip the Mac 'n' Cheese first into the seasoned flour, then into the egg and milk mixture, and finally into the seasoned breadcrumbs. Repeat the process until all of the bites are breaded.

- Heat the oil over a medium-high heat to around 180°C/356°F. Carefully place the Mac 'n' Cheese Bites in the oil and fry for around 2–3 minutes or until they take on a golden colour. Remove from the oil and drain off any excess oil on kitchen paper. Allow to stand for 1–2 minutes before serving on a warmed plate.

FRIED PICKLES

Serves 4

These little pickle fritters are so quick and easy to make, perfect for snacking! Pop-up bars and restaurants across America often serve customers a complimentary bowl of these tangy, crispy pickles, no doubt rewarded in turn by thirsty customers who take to ordering another round of drinks to wash them down! Serve with ketchup or Burger Sauce (page 224).

   120g plain flour
   60g cornflour
   ¼ teaspoon garlic powder
   Pinch of chilli powder
   ¼ teaspoon sea salt
   ¼ teaspoon black pepper
   1 tablespoon vegetable oil
   350ml any good-quality beer or lager
   1 x 680g jar of whole pickled gherkins
   Vegetable oil for deep-frying
   1–2 tablespoons plain flour, seasoned with a little sea salt
      and black pepper

- To a bowl, add plain flour, cornflour, garlic powder, chilli powder, sea salt and black pepper. Mix well. Add the vegetable oil and beer or lager and mix well until a smooth batter is formed. Add a little more if necessary until the batter has the consistency of single cream.

- Slice the gherkins into bite-sized pieces. Heat the oil to around 180°C/356°F. Meanwhile transfer the seasoned flour to a plate and dip each gherkin piece in it to coat. Dip the floured gherkin bites into the prepared batter and place carefully in the hot oil. Fry the pickles for 2–3 minutes or until the batter is golden and crisp and drain off any excess oil on kitchen paper.

- Arrange the fried pickles on a warmed serving plate and serve with your favourite dipping sauce.

HUSH PUPPIES

Serves 2

It's said by some that Hush Puppies were invented by hunts-men and fishermen, who used the snacks to keep their dogs quiet for a while. After battering their own food, scraps would be fried and dished out to the dogs, who immediately busied themselves and tidied up the leftovers. Nowadays, Hush Puppies are a popular snack across the whole of America, but particularly in the South and wherever seafood is served.

1 small onion, peeled and finely chopped
1 egg
3 tablespoons caster sugar
60g self-raising flour
60g cornmeal
¼ teaspoon garlic powder
Pinch of cayenne pepper
Pinch of sea salt
2–3 tablespoons milk
Vegetable oil for deep-frying
Chopped crispy bacon and freshly sliced spring onions, to serve (optional)

- To a bowl, add the onion, egg and caster sugar. Mix well. Add the self-raising flour, cornmeal, garlic powder, cayenne pepper, sea salt and milk. Mix thoroughly, adding a little more cornmeal or milk, if necessary, until the batter reaches the consistency of a thick cake mix.

- Heat the oil to around 180°C/356°F. Using two teaspoons, carefully drop teaspoon-sized amounts of batter into the hot oil. Fry in batches for around 3–4 minutes or until golden on all sides.

- Drain off any excess oil on kitchen paper and arrange the Hush Puppies on a warmed serving plate. Top with crispy bacon and sliced spring onions, if desired, and serve.

POUTINE/DISCO FRIES

Serves 2

All around the world, people of different races and cultures have decided unanimously that fried potatoes topped with cheese and gravy or sauce is a good thing indeed! The Canadian dish, Poutine, is a delicious mix of crispy fries, creamy melted curds and flavoursome gravy and can be adapted in various ways. The US state of New Jersey is home to 'Disco Fries', a similar dish made with mozzarella cheese, while the UK's Chips 'n' Cheese is another cousin of the same dish. Add a generous portion of Beef Chilli (page 22) and you have Chilli Cheese Fries! Whatever your chosen combo, you can be sure it's going to be good!

4 large Maris Piper or King Edward potatoes
Vegetable oil for deep-frying
Sea salt to season, to taste
Cheese curds, Twarog (Polish-style curd cheese) and
    mozzarella cheese, to serve

Gravy
2 tablespoons oyster sauce
1 teaspoon light soy sauce
1 teaspoon dark soy sauce
2 teaspoon tomato ketchup
1 teaspoon vegetable oil

1 small onion, peeled and sliced

1 tablespoon rice wine

100ml beef stock

2 teaspoons potato flour or cornflour, mixed with 1 tablespoon of water

Dash of toasted sesame oil

- Make the gravy: To a small bowl, add oyster sauce, light and dark soy sauces and tomato ketchup. Mix well.

- Heat 1 teaspoon of vegetable oil over a medium heat. Add the sliced onion and stir-fry for 2–3 minutes. Pour in the rice wine and stir-fry for a further 30 seconds. Add the prepared sauce and beef stock. Simmer for 3–4 minutes or until slightly reduced. Add the potato flour or cornflour and water mix and keep stirring until the gravy thickens. Add the toasted sesame oil, turn off the heat and set aside until needed. The gravy can be reheated as needed and will keep well in the refrigerator, covered, for 2 days.

- Peel the potatoes and slice into 1cm fries. Rinse thoroughly in plenty of water for 1–2 minutes to remove the starch. Fill a large saucepan with water and bring to the boil. Add the potatoes and simmer for 3–4 minutes. Drain thoroughly, pat dry with kitchen paper and set aside to cool.

- Heat the oil for deep-frying to around 130°C/266°F. Carefully place the potatoes in the hot oil and fry for 5–6 minutes or until just softened but not coloured. Remove from the pan and set aside aside until ready to use.

- To finish off, heat the oil to around 180°C/356°F. Fry the potatoes for 2–3 minutes or until crispy and golden. Remove the fries from the pan, drain off any excess oil on kitchen paper and arrange on a warmed serving plate. Season to taste with sea salt.

- Top the chips with cheese. Wait 1–2 minutes (if you can resist!) for the cheese to melt a little and serve with warmed gravy on the side to pour over the top.

FALAFEL

Serves 2

A street food classic, falafel is a Middle Eastern vegetarian dish of spiced chickpeas and/or fava beans, fried until crisp and often served with pitta breads and salad. The prepared falafel mix can also be used to make Veggie Burgers (see Box opposite).

1 x 400g tin chickpeas
1 small onion, peeled and roughly chopped
1 garlic clove, peeled and roughly chopped
1 teaspoon cumin powder
1 teaspoon coriander powder
¼ teaspoon allspice
½ teaspoon mild chilli powder
Pinch of nutmeg
Pinch of ground ginger
½ teaspoon baking powder
½ teaspoon sea salt
¼ teaspoon black pepper
Handful of fresh coriander leaves, chopped, plus extra to garnish
3–4 tablespoons gram (chickpea flour, also known as 'besan') flour
Vegetable oil for deep-frying
Sriracha sauce (from supermarkets), to serve

- Drain the chickpeas, rinse in cold water and drain again.

- To a blender bowl add the onion, garlic, two-thirds of the chickpeas, cumin powder, coriander powder, allspice, chilli powder, nutmeg, ground ginger, baking powder, sea salt and black pepper. Blend to a paste.

- Add the remaining chickpeas and pulse 2–3 times to incorporate into the mix. Pour the falafel mix into a bowl and add the gram flour, mixing well until the mixture is thick and easily drops from a teaspoon (add more chickpea flour, if necessary).

- Heat the oil to around 180°C/356°F. Using two teaspoons, carefully drop teaspoon-sized amounts of the mixture into the hot oil. Fry the falafel in batches for around 2–3 minutes or until golden and crispy. Drain off any excess oil on kitchen paper and arrange the falafel in a warmed serving bowl. Serve garnished with a little extra fresh coriander and sriracha sauce.

Veggie Burgers

To prepare Veggie Burgers from the falafel mix, lay out a sheet of baking paper and press out a large handful of falafel mixture until a large thin patty is formed. Repeat until all of the mixture is used (the recipe above will make 2 large burgers). Layer the shaped patties between baking paper and chill for an hour before frying. This makes it much easier to lift them cleanly from the baking paper before frying.

To cook the Veggie Burgers, heat the vegetable oil for deep-frying to 180°C/356°F. Carefully place the patties in the hot oil and fry for 3–4 minutes or until cooked through and golden. Remove from the pan, drain off any excess oil on kitchen paper and serve in toasted burger buns with Hot Sauce (page 227).

5

STIR-FRIES, SOUPS & CURRIES

Prior preparation prevents poor performance they say, and when it comes to stir-fry dishes this is most certainly true. With ingredients cut to size, marinated, arranged and ready, the dish comes together in a matter of moments in a blazing-hot wok set over a high heat.

Stir-fry cooking often involves a flurry of fast-paced activity as the chef tosses and stirs all manner of ingredients into the wok. Blink and you'll miss it, the leaping flames and sizzling sounds adding a performance aspect to proceedings as hungry locals and visitors gather round to enjoy the show and, of course, the end result.

As well as providing entertainment for both the cook and the hungry guests, stir-fry cooking allows us to prepare dishes in a healthy manner with just a little oil and plenty of fresh vegetables. Flash-frying ingredients for just a few minutes ensures the meat remains juicy and the vegetables retain many of their nutrients and health benefits.

When cooking for several people, stir-frying allows for customisation of dishes according to individual tastes. Cooking each small portion to order means the temperature in the pan stays hot at all times, resulting in food which has a delicious smoky flavour.

Soups and curry dishes are perfect comfort food, big on flavour with little effort, perfect for both street food chefs and home cooks. Using fragrant ingredients such as fish sauce, rice wine, aromatic spices, etc. enables the cook to turn simple chicken or vegetable stocks (even made from cubes) into something very special indeed. If things weren't positive enough already, soups and curry sauces also offer good potential for healthy eating as the broths and liquids fill us up and enable us to feel fuller for longer.

PAD KRA POW GAI (HOLY BASIL CHICKEN)

Serves 1

Literally translated as 'fried holy basil chicken', this dish can be made with holy basil or Thai basil, with differing but equally excellent results. Thai basil is sweet whereas holy basil is on the spicier side. If neither is available, a mix of fresh coriander and fresh mint leaves also provides a tasty dish.

½ small red onion, peeled and sliced
3 garlic cloves, peeled and roughly chopped
2–3 Thai chillies (see also page 33)
1 teaspoon light soy sauce
1 teaspoon dark soy sauce
1 teaspoon oyster sauce
Dash of fish sauce
75ml light chicken stock or water
Pinch of white pepper
2 skinless, boneless chicken thigh fillets (150g total weight)
1 teaspoon rice wine
½ teaspoon sesame oil
½ teaspoon potato flour or cornflour
1 tablespoon vegetable oil
Handful of sliced green beans
4–5 Thai basil leaves
Handful of fresh coriander leaves, chopped

Thai Sticky Rice (page 169) and 1 crispy fried egg per
person, to serve (see Box opposite)

- To the bowl of a pestle and mortar add the onion, garlic
  and Thai chillies. Pound to a rough paste and set aside.

- Add light and dark soy sauce, oyster sauce, fish sauce,
  chicken stock or water and white pepper to a bowl to make
  a sauce. Set aside.

- Trim any excess fat from the chicken thighs and slice into
  thin strips. Place the chicken in a bowl and add rice wine,
  sesame oil and potato flour or cornflour. Mix well and set
  aside.

- Heat a little of the vegetable oil in a wok or large frying pan
  set over a medium-high heat. Add the chicken and allow to
  cook, untouched, for 1 minute. Stir-fry for 3–4 minutes or
  until just cooked. Remove and set aside.

- Wipe out the wok or frying pan with kitchen paper and add
  another touch of oil. Add the green beans and stir-fry for 2
  minutes. Add the onion, garlic and chilli paste and stir-fry
  for 2 minutes or until fragrant. Return the cooked chicken
  slices to the pan. Add the prepared sauce mixture and
  reduce the heat to low. Simmer for 2 minutes or until the
  sauce thickens a little.

- Add the Thai basil leaves and fresh coriander to the pan
  and turn off the heat. Mix once more before transferring

the chicken and vegetables to a warmed serving dish. Serve with Thai Sticky Rice and a crispy fried egg per person.

Crispy Fried Eggs

Crispy fried eggs are a common topping in Thai street food. Cooked using lots of hot oil, the egg puffs up and cooks quickly, adding indulgence to already flavourful sauces and rice dishes.

Heat 100ml vegetable oil in a frying pan set over a medium-high heat. Crack an egg into the pan and fry for 2–3 minutes, spooning hot oil over the top of the egg as it cooks. The yolk should remain slightly soft and the white a little crispy on the edges. Drain off any excess oil and serve.

Top your Pad Kra Pow Gai with a crispy fried egg, burst the yolk and mix through both the sauce and the rice.

FIREWORK CHICKEN

Serves 1

Slightly sweet, definitely spicy and full of fresh vegetables, the sauce used in this dish tastes more than the sum of its parts. Equally delicious made with king prawns in place of chicken.

1 skinless, boneless chicken breast fillet (113g)
1 teaspoon rice wine
1 teaspoon toasted sesame oil
½ teaspoon potato flour or cornflour
1 tablespoon vegetable oil
1 onion, peeled and roughly chopped
¼ red pepper, deseeded and roughly chopped
¼ green pepper, deseeded and roughly chopped
2–3 dried red chillies
4–5 sugar snap peas
½ teaspoon Garlic & Ginger Paste (page 228)
1 spring onion, trimmed, peeled and finely sliced, and a handful of fresh coriander, finely chopped, to garnish
Simple Boiled Rice (page 168), shichimi and a wedge of lime, to serve

Sauce
1 tablespoon oyster sauce
½ teaspoon light soy sauce
½ teaspoon dark soy sauce

1 teaspoon ketchup

1 teaspoon sriracha sauce (from supermarkets)

½ teaspoon sweet chilli sauce

1 teaspoon rice wine vinegar

2 teaspoons soft brown sugar

2 teaspoons lime juice

Pinch of white pepper

50ml water or chicken stock

1 teaspoon potato or corn flour, mixed with 1 tablespoon water

- To make the sauce, add the oyster sauce, light and dark soy sauces, ketchup, sriracha sauce, sweet chilli sauce, rice wine vinegar, brown sugar, lime juice, white pepper and water or chicken stock to a bowl. Mix well and set aside.

- Trim any excess fat from the chicken breast fillet and cut into 5–6 long strips. Place in a bowl and add the rice wine, toasted sesame oil and potato flour or cornflour. Mix well and set aside.

- Heat half the oil in a wok or large frying pan set over a high heat. Add the chicken strips and cook, untouched, for 1 minute. Stir-fry the chicken for a further 3–4 minutes or until golden and just cooked. Remove from the pan and set aside.

- Wipe the pan clean with kitchen paper and add the remaining oil. Add the onion, red and green pepper, dried red chillies and sugar snap peas. Stir-fry for 1–2 minutes. Add the Garlic & Ginger Paste and stir-fry for a further 30 seconds.

- Return the chicken slices to the pan. Add the prepared sauce and cook for 1–2 minutes or until the sauce reduces. Turn the heat down low, add the potato flour or cornflour and water mix and stir-fry for 1 minute to thicken.

- Transfer the Firecracker Chicken to a large warmed serving bowl. Garnish with spring onions and freshly chopped coriander. Serve with Simple Boiled Rice topped with shichimi and a wedge of lime.

CRISPY VOLCANO CHICKEN WITH SWEET CHILLI TAMARIND SAUCE

Serves 2

Potato flour or cornflour are perfect for coating the chicken before frying, creating a crisp and slightly chewy crust on the meat. Combined with a sweet chilli sauce made a little sour with tamarind, the results are spectacular. I first tried this Thai dish in a New Jersey restaurant, where the owner, Mama, offers a wide variety of deliciously spicy dishes.

2 tablespoons oyster sauce
1 teaspoon light soy sauce
1 teaspoon dark soy sauce
1 tablespoon tamarind paste (see Box below)
1 tablespoon sweet chilli sauce
2 chicken breast fillets (each around 113g weight)
2 teaspoons rice wine
2 teaspoons toasted sesame oil
1 egg
7–8 tablespoons potato flour or cornflour
1 teaspoon vegetable oil, plus extra for deep-frying
1 onion, peeled and chopped
Handful of sprouting broccoli
Handful of fresh coriander leaves, finely chopped, to
   garnish
Rice or noodles, to serve

- To make the Sweet Chilli Tamarind Sauce, add the oyster sauce, light and dark soy sauces, tamarind paste and sweet chilli sauce to a bowl. Mix well and set aside.

- Trim any excess fat from the chicken breasts and cut into bite-sized pieces. Pour the rice wine and sesame oil into a large bowl. Mix well, add the chicken pieces and combine.

- Whisk the egg in separate small bowl. Add around half of the beaten egg to the chicken pieces and mix well. Add the potato flour or cornflour to the chicken and mix well once again.

- Heat oil for deep-frying to around 180°C/356°F. Carefully place the floured chicken pieces in the hot oil and fry for around 5–6 minutes or until crispy and golden. Remove from the pan, drain off any excess oil on kitchen paper and set aside.

- Heat 1 teaspoon of vegetable oil in a wok or large frying pan set over a medium heat. Add the onion and sprouting broccoli; stir-fry for 2–3 minutes. Add the fried chicken pieces and the prepared sauce. Mix well for 1–2 minutes until the sauce is slightly thickened and the chicken is well coated in the sauce.

- Arrange the Volcano Chicken in a warmed serving bowl, garnish with fresh coriander leaves and serve with Simple Boiled Rice (page 168) or Singapore Street Noodles (page 184).

Tamarind Paste

Dried tamarind pulp stores well and so making your own tamarind paste as and when you need it can be cost-effective and convenient. Supermarkets now stock readymade tamarind paste, which provides good results, albeit at more expense. To make your own from a dried tamarind block (available in larger supermarkets), place 25g of dried tamarind pulp into a heatproof bowl, cover with 50ml boiling water and let stand for 30 minutes. Press the paste through a sieve, cool and then cover and store in the refrigerator for up to 1 week.

GUNPOWDER CHICKEN

Serves 2

Rich and full of flavour, this chicken is firmly camped in the hot and spicy category, with just enough sweetness to leave you coming back for more.

2 tablespoons dark soy sauce
1 teaspoon light soy sauce
1 tablespoon rice wine
1 tablespoon balsamic vinegar
1 teaspoon soft brown sugar
Pinch of Chinese five-spice
Dash of toasted sesame oil or Chilli Oil (page 230)
2 tablespoons water
4–6 skinless, boneless chicken thigh fillets (450g weight)
1 tablespoon vegetable oil
2–4 dried bird's eye chillies
2 spring onions, trimmed, peeled and sliced
1 tablespoon Roasted peanuts (see Box opposite)
Potato flour/water for thickening (see method)
Simple Boiled Rice (page 168) or noodles, to serve

• To a bowl add dark and light soy sauce, rice wine, balsamic vinegar, brown sugar, Chinese five-spice, sesame or Chilli Oil and water. Mix well.

- Trim any excess fat from the chicken thighs and cut into bite-sized pieces. Add ½ tablespoon of the prepared sauce and mix well. Set aside to marinate for 30 minutes.

- Heat the vegetable oil in a wok or large frying pan set over a high heat. Carefully add the chicken pieces to the pan and cook, untouched, for 1 minute. Stir-fry for a further 3–4 minutes or until golden and cooked through. Remove from the pan and set aside.

- Add the bird's eye chillies, spring onions and roasted peanuts to the pan. Stir-fry for 1 minute. Add the prepared sauce and simmer for 2 minutes or until the sauce reduces slightly. Thicken the sauce with as much potato flour/water as necessary to achieve the desired consistency.

- Transfer the Gunpowder Chicken to a serving plate and serve with Simple Boiled Rice.

Roasted Nuts

This simple roasting method can be used with cashews or peanuts, which are ideal for crushing. Heat a wok or large frying pan set over a medium heat. When hot, add 3–4 tablespoons raw nuts and stir-fry for 2–3 minutes in the dry pan until toasted and aromatic. Transfer from the pan to a food-safe container and allow to cool completely. Crush roughly in a pestle and mortar and serve with Thai stir-fry or noodle dishes.

PRAWN LAKSA

Serves 2

Rich and indulgent, king prawns, coconut and coriander combine to great effect in this noodle soup. Whilst rice noodles are more commonly used in Laksa dishes, the texture of egg noodles stands up well to the strong flavours in this dish.

1 x 83g nest udon noodles
1 teaspoon coconut oil
¼ red pepper, deseeded and finely chopped
1 spring onion, trimmed, peeled and finely sliced
1 teaspoon Garlic & Ginger Paste (page 228)
1 red Thai chilli, deseeded and finely sliced (see also page 33)
100g raw king prawns
100ml coconut milk
100ml chicken stock
Handful of fresh coriander leaves, finely chopped, to garnish

- Place the noodle nest in a heatproof bowl, cover with boiling water and leave to stand for 3–4 minutes. Separate the noodles with a fork. Pour the noodles through a sieve and drain the water. Rinse briefly with cold water, drain once more and set aside.

- Heat the coconut oil in a saucepan set over a medium heat. Add the red pepper and stir-fry for 1 minute. Add the spring onion, Garlic & Ginger Paste and red Thai chilli. Stir-fry for a further minute.

- Add the king prawns and stir-fry for 2 minutes or until they are just beginning to turn a little pink. Add the coconut milk and chicken stock. Bring the mixture to the boil, reduce the heat to low and simmer for 3–4 minutes until the broth is slightly thick and the prawns are pink and cooked through.

- Add the prepared noodles to the pan and simmer for 1 minute to warm through. Ladle the Laksa into warmed serving bowls, garnish with fresh coriander and serve.

BAKSO (INDONESIAN MEATBALL SOUP)

Serves 1

This combination dish makes excellent use of leftover meats and vegetables and is perfect when cooking for a lot of people at once. After preparing a cold noodle salad, the hot sriracha sauce and piping-hot beef broth and meatballs come together to form a spectacular and spicy meal. Kecap manis is sweeter than soy sauce and offers a beautifully balanced flavour when added to soups and sauces. If you can't find it, dark soy sauce provides a suitable alternative, perhaps with a pinch of soft brown sugar for added sweetness.

300ml beef stock

Dash of light soy sauce

1 teaspoon kecap manis (Indonesian sweet soy sauce, see page 229)

Pinch of white pepper

7–8 good-quality beef meatballs

1 spring onion, trimmed, peeled and sliced

Sriracha sauce (from supermarkets), to serve

Noodle Salad

1 nest egg noodles

1 teaspoon Chilli Oil (page 230)

½ teaspoon kecap manis (Indonesian sweet soy sauce, see page 229)

½ teaspoon light soy sauce
Pinch of white pepper
Handful of any cooked and cooled leftover roast meat
1 spring onion, trimmed, peeled and sliced

- To make the salad, place the noodle nest in a heatproof bowl, cover with boiling water and leave to stand for 3–4 minutes. Separate the noodles with a fork. Pour the noodles through a sieve and drain the water. Rinse briefly with cold water, drain once more and place in a large serving bowl. Top with Chilli Oil, kecap manis, light soy sauce and white pepper. Arrange the cooked meat on top, garnish with spring onion and set aside.

- To a saucepan add beef stock and bring to the boil. Reduce the heat to low, add the light soy sauce, kecap manis and white pepper. Simmer the broth for 8–10 minutes.

- Cook the meatballs according to package instructions and add to the simmering broth along with the sliced spring onion. Serve the Bakso alongside the prepared noodle salad with sriracha sauce on the side.

SRIRACHA CHICKEN NOODLE SOUP

Serves 4

This soup may be served without the sriracha sauce for those who prefer a milder flavour. With sriracha added, however, it takes on a new dimension – spicy, zingy and instant good-mood food!

2 egg noodle nests
3 chicken breast fillets (around 113g each)
Pinch of sea salt
¼ teaspoon white pepper
1 tablespoon rice wine
1 teaspoon vegetable oil
750ml chicken stock
1 teaspoon kecap manis (Indonesian sweet soy sauce, see
   page 229)
1 tablespoon light soy sauce
2 teaspoons dark soy sauce
½ teaspoon garlic powder
200g sweetcorn, tinned or frozen
3 teaspoons sriracha sauce (from supermarkets)
Handful of fresh coriander, finely chopped

- Place the noodle nests in a heatproof bowl, cover with boiling water and leave to stand for 3–4 minutes. Separate the noodles with a fork. Pour the noodles through a sieve and drain the water. Rinse briefly with cold water, drain once more and set aside.

- Trim any excess fat from the chicken breast fillets and cut into small thin pieces. Place in a bowl and add sea salt, white pepper and rice wine. Mix well.

- Heat the vegetable oil in a large stockpot. Add the chicken pieces and stir-fry for 1–2 minutes. Add the chicken stock, kecap manis, light and dark soy sauces and garlic powder. Mix well, bring to the boil, reduce the heat to low and simmer for 10–12 minutes.

- Add the sweetcorn and prepared egg noodles. Mix well and simmer for a further 2–3 minutes. Ladle the chicken, vegetables and noodles into warmed serving bowls. Add the sriracha sauce, sprinkle with coriander and serve.

PORK PHO WITH EGG NOODLES

Serves 4

Pho is a serious business and many street vendors pride themselves on low and slow-cooked stocks packed full of flavour.
When time is short, however, good-quality stocks can be
transformed into something very special indeed with the
addition of some aromatic flavours.

1 nest egg noodles
1 teaspoon vegetable oil
250g pork mince
1 teaspoon Garlic & Ginger Paste (page 228)
1½ teaspoons chilli bean sauce
½ teaspoon Chinese five-spice
Pinch of white pepper
800ml chicken stock
Dash of fish sauce
2 teaspoons light soy sauce
1 teaspoon dark soy sauce
1 teaspoon rice wine vinegar
Pinch of sugar
Handful of sliced green beans or sugar snap peas (optional)
Handful of fresh coriander leaves, finely chopped, to
    garnish
1 chilli pepper, deseeded and finely sliced (see also page
    33), to garnish

1–2 spring onions, trimmed, peeled and finely sliced, to
   garnish
Dash of toasted sesame oil
Sriracha sauce (from supermarkets), to serve

- Place the noodle nest in a heatproof bowl, cover with boiling water and leave to stand for 3–4 minutes. Separate the
  noodles with a fork. Pour the noodles through a sieve and
  drain the water. Rinse briefly with cold water, drain once
  more and set aside.

- Heat the vegetable oil in a large saucepan set over a
  medium heat. Add the pork mince and stir-fry for 2–3
  minutes or until broken up and browned. Add the Garlic &
  Ginger Paste, chilli bean sauce, Chinese five-spice and
  white pepper. Mix well.

- Add the chicken stock, fish sauce, light and dark soy sauces,
  rice wine vinegar and sugar. Mix well. Add the green beans
  or sugar snap peas, if desired. Bring to the boil, reduce the
  heat to low and simmer for 8–10 minutes. Add the prepared
  noodles and mix well. Simmer for a further 2 minutes or
  until the noodles are piping hot.

- Ladle the Pho into warmed serving bowls. Garnish with
  fresh coriander, chilli and spring onions. Finish off with a
  dash of toasted sesame oil and serve with the sriracha
  sauce.

RED PORK COCONUT CURRY

Serves 4

Rich and indulgent with coconut and peanuts, this is the ultimate Thai curry! Separate the stalks and leaves from fresh coriander and use the stalks to begin the curry and the leaves to garnish.

2 teaspoons coconut oil

6 spring onions, trimmed, peeled and finely sliced

Handful of fresh coriander stems, finely sliced

1 lemongrass stalk, finely chopped

2 kaffir lime leaves

½ red pepper, deseeded and finely diced

¼ teaspoon Garlic & Ginger Paste (page 228)

400g pork loin fillet, finely sliced

4 tablespoons Thai red curry paste

2 teaspoons light soy sauce

2 teaspoons dark soy sauce

400ml coconut milk

4 tablespoons peanut butter

50ml water

200g tinned or frozen sweetcorn

Handful of mangetout or sliced green beans

1 tablespoon fish sauce

Juice of 1 lime

Handful of fresh coriander leaves, finely chopped, to
    serve

- Heat the coconut oil over a medium heat in a wok or large frying pan. Add the sliced spring onions and coriander stems. Stir-fry for 2 minutes. Add the lemongrass stalk and kaffir lime leaves. Mix well then add the red pepper and Garlic & Ginger Paste. Stir-fry for 2 minutes.

- Add the sliced pork and stir-fry for 2–3 minutes or until sealed and golden. Add the Thai red curry paste, light and dark soy sauces, coconut milk, peanut butter and water. Mix well, bring to the boil, reduce the heat to low and simmer for 15 minutes.

- Add the tinned or frozen sweetcorn and mangetout or sliced green beans to the pan. Simmer for 5 minutes. Stir in the fish sauce and lime juice. Ladle the curry into warmed serving dishes, garnish with fresh coriander leaves and serve.

CHANA MASALA (CHICKPEA CURRY)

Serves 2

This tasty curry can be enjoyed immediately when cooked but is actually best eaten at room temperature, accompanied of course by some crispy poppadoms, chapatti bread and chilli pickle. In this dish the chilli is not deseeded as the tomatoes work well with it to provide a flavour that is just slightly hot.

2 salad tomatoes, quartered
1 red onion, peeled and quartered
2 teaspoons Garlic & Ginger Paste (page 228)
1 green chilli (see also page 33)
2 tablespoons water
2 teaspoons cumin powder
1 teaspoon coriander powder
1 teaspoon turmeric
1 teaspoon garam masala
Pinch of mild chilli powder
½ teaspoon dried fenugreek leaves (also known as methi)
Pinch of sea salt
1 tablespoon vegetable oil
1 x 400g tin chickpeas, rinsed and drained
1 tablespoon lemon juice
Handful of fresh coriander leaves, finely chopped
Crispy poppadoms, chapatti bread and chilli pickle, to
    serve

- To the bowl of a blender, add the tomatoes, red onion, Garlic & Ginger Paste, green chilli and 1 tablespoon water. Blend well and set aside.

- To another bowl, add the cumin powder, coriander powder, turmeric, garam masala, chilli powder, dried fenugreek leaves, sea salt and the remaining water. Mix well and set aside.

- Heat the oil in a saucepan set over a low heat. Add the prepared spice mix and stir-fry for 1 minute or until the spices foam in the pan. Add the chickpeas and mix well. Add the prepared blended sauce. Bring to the boil, reduce the heat to low and simmer for 5–6 minutes or until the sauce thickens to the desired consistency. Turn off the heat, add the lemon juice and fresh coriander leaves and mix once more.

- Serve the Chana Masala immediately or at room temperature with crispy poppadoms, chapatti bread and chilli pickle on the side.

PAV BHAJI (INDIAN VEGETABLE BUTTER CURRY)

Serves 8

This light, vegetable curry dish can be found all over India and was reputedly invented to appease factory owners who were unhappy to see staff return from lunch feeling tired and sleepy after a heavy meal. Instead, this light vegetable-based curry dish was created. As is typical of many Indian street foods, it's traditionally served with Pav (soft white bread rolls). Brioche rolls also work perfectly, adding another buttery element, which combines well with the curry.

1 large potato (Maris Piper or King Edward)
½ cauliflower, trimmed and roughly chopped
100g frozen garden peas
2 teaspoons coconut oil
2 teaspoons salted butter, plus 2–3 teaspoons salted butter to finish the curry
2 onions, peeled and finely chopped
½ green pepper, deseeded and finely chopped
1 teaspoon Garlic & Ginger Paste (page 228)
2 salad tomatoes, finely chopped
¼ teaspoon sea salt, plus extra for seasoning
½ teaspoon chilli powder
¼ teaspoon turmeric
1 tablespoon pav bhaji masala (see Box page 166)
Pinch of dried fenugreek leaves (also known as methi)

400ml water

8 small soft white bread rolls or brioche rolls and a little
oil or salted butter, to serve

1 lemon, cut into 8 wedges, to garnish

1 onion, peeled and finely chopped, to garnish

Handful of fresh coriander leaves, finely chopped, to
garnish

- Peel the potato if desired (it isn't necessary), dice and add
to a large saucepan. Add the chopped cauliflower, cover
with water and season with a little salt. Bring to the boil,
reduce the heat to medium and simmer for 10 minutes
until the potatoes and cauliflower are just beginning to
soften. Add the frozen peas, return to the boil and cook for
a further 2 minutes. Drain the water, mash the vegetables
roughly and set aside.

- Heat the coconut oil and 2 teaspoons salted butter in a wok
or large frying pan. Add the onions and stir-fry for 2
minutes. Add the green pepper and stir-fry for a further 2
minutes. Add the Garlic & Ginger Paste and stir-fry for a
further minute.

- Add the chopped tomatoes and sea salt. Stir-fry for 2
minutes. Add the chilli powder, turmeric, pav bhaji masala
and dried fenugreek leaves. Stir-fry for a further 2 minutes.

- Add the water and mix well. Stir in the prepared potato,
cauliflower and peas. Bring to the boil, reduce the heat to

low and cook for around 20 minutes or until the curry reaches the desired consistency, mashing often to break up the vegetable mix. As the curry is almost cooked, add the remaining 2–3 teaspoons salted butter. The finished curry should be fairly thick and the vegetables mashed into the sauce until no large pieces remain.

- Slice the bread rolls in half and spread a little oil or salted butter on to the insides. Toast briefly in a hot pan set over a medium heat for 2–3 minutes until toasted and warm.

- Ladle the curry into warmed serving dishes and serve garnished with lemon wedges, finely chopped raw onion and fresh coriander leaves. Stir another small piece of butter into the curry just before serving, if desired. This is a nice touch visually as it melts slowly into the curry but it also adds an indulgently creamy and rich finish to the dish. Serve with the toasted bread rolls.

Perfectly Spiced

Pav bhaji masala is widely available from specialist Indian grocery stores and online. A mix of coriander, cumin, cloves, cinnamon and more, many supermarket tikka-style curry powders have a similar composition and will work well as an alternative.

6

RICE & NOODLES

Sometimes only a steaming hot plate of rice or noodles will do. The dishes in this chapter are focused on those that, rather than being offered as an accompaniment to a main dish, instead offer rice and noodles as part of the main show.

Most dried egg noodle products advise boiling the noodles for 3–4 minutes. This can often make the noodles too soft, particularly if they are intended for use in stir-fry dishes. In most cases, simply covering the noodles with boiling water and allowing to stand for 3–4 minutes before rinsing and draining is sufficient.

Supermarkets now carry a wide range of pre-prepared rice packs, which are very handy when it comes to stir-frying in a hurry. That said, it's certainly more cost-effective to prepare your own boiled rice and chill it for 24 hours for use in fried rice dishes the next day.

SIMPLE BOILED RICE

Makes 1 portion

Fragrant basmati rice is perfect as a side dish with any stir-fry or curry dish. This recipe is foolproof and ensures your rice comes out perfect every time!

100g good-quality basmati rice (dry weight)
200ml water

- Place the basmati rice in a large bowl and cover with plenty of cold water. Set aside for 1 hour, changing the water 3–4 times during this time. Rinse the rice thoroughly through a sieve until the water runs clear. Drain thoroughly and empty the soaked rice into a large saucepan.

- Add the water to the saucepan and bring to the boil over a high heat. Once boiling, reduce the heat to low, cover with a lid and simmer, untouched, for 14 minutes. Turn off the heat and allow the rice to stand for a further 10 minutes. Fluff up with a fork before serving.

Variation
For fried rice, cool the cooked rice quickly, place in a food-safe container and set aside in the refrigerator for 24 hours before use in fried rice dishes.

THAI STICKY RICE

Makes 1 portion

So simple, yet so fragrant, Thai Sticky Rice has a mild, slightly sweet flavour and is perfect as a side dish to accompany flavourful and spicy curries or stir-fries. Topped with sweetened coconut milk, it also makes a beautifully indulgent dessert (page 256). The recipe can be increased provided the rice/water ratios are consistent.

100g Thai sticky rice
150ml water
Fresh coriander leaves, to garnish

- In a large bowl, place the Thai sticky rice and cover with a generous amount of water. Soak the rice for around 1 hour, changing the water two to three times.

- Drain the soaked rice and rinse until the water runs clear. Drain again and place the rice in a saucepan. Add 150ml water and bring to the boil over a high heat. Once boiling, reduce the heat to low, cover with a lid and simmer for 14 minutes.

- Spoon the cooked rice into a mould or small bowl and pack tightly. Turn the rice out onto a warmed serving plate, garnish with fresh coriander leaves and serve alongside your favourite Thai dishes. The cooked and cooled rice is perfect with Chennai Chicken Fried Rice (page 173) and Nasi Goreng (page 175).

NYC-STYLE CHICKEN OVER RICE

Serves 2

New York City plays host to a huge number of 'halal' carts, where Jeera (Cumin) Chicken Over Rice with Hot Sauce & Garlic Sauce is a favourite amongst tourists and residents alike.

½ teaspoon garlic powder
Pinch of ginger powder
¼ teaspoon cumin powder
¼ teaspoon paprika
¼ teaspoon smoked paprika
Pinch of allspice
½ teaspoon dried oregano
Pinch of dried thyme
¼ teaspoon sea salt
Pinch of black pepper
1 tablespoon tomato ketchup
1 teaspoon virgin olive oil
1 teaspoon distilled white vinegar
4–6 skinless, boneless chicken thigh fillets (around 450g total weight)
Vegetable oil for frying
100ml light chicken stock
Garlic Sauce (page 226), Hot Sauce (page 227), toasted pitta breads and mixed salad leaves, to serve

Rice

200g basmati rice

400ml water

½ teaspoon turmeric

¼ teaspoon cumin powder

¼ teaspoon sea salt

- To a bowl, add the garlic powder, ginger powder, cumin powder, paprika, smoked paprika, allspice, dried oregano, dried thyme, sea salt, black pepper, tomato ketchup, olive oil and distilled white vinegar. Mix well and set aside.

- Trim any excess fat from the chicken thigh fillets. Add the fillets to a food-safe bowl and pour over the prepared marinade. Cover and set aside in the refrigerator for 2 hours. Remove from the refrigerator 30 minutes before cooking.

- Prepare the rice: Soak the rice as described on page 168. Place the soaked and drained rice in a large saucepan, add the water, turmeric, cumin powder and sea salt. Bring to the boil over a high heat. Once boiling, reduce the heat to low, cover with a lid and simmer, untouched, for 14 minutes. After 14 minutes, turn off the heat and allow the rice to stand for a further 10 minutes. Fluff up with a fork before serving.

- Heat the vegetable oil in a large frying pan set over a high heat. Add the chicken thighs and cook, untouched, for 2 minutes or until golden. Flip the chicken and cook for a further 2 minutes or until golden on all sides.

- Reduce the heat to low, add the stock and simmer the chicken for 7–8 minutes or until cooked through. Remove from the pan to a chopping board. Increase the heat in the pan to high and let the liquid reduce for 2–3 minutes. Meanwhile shred the chicken into very small pieces using two forks or a pair of kitchen scissors.

- Return the shredded chicken to the pan, increase the heat to high and mix well. Stir-fry for 2–3 minutes, or until the chicken is nicely charred.

- Arrange the cooked chicken and rice on a warmed serving platter. Top with Garlic Sauce and Hot Sauce. Serve with toasted pitta breads and mixed salad leaves.

CHENNAI CHICKEN FRIED RICE

Serves 1

This Indo-Chinese fusion is a meal in itself or can be served in smaller portions as a side dish.

1 portion Chicken 65 (page 109)
1 tablespoon vegetable oil
1 egg
½ small onion, peeled and finely chopped
1 green chilli, deseeded and finely sliced (see also page 33)
3–4 cabbage leaves, finely chopped
1 portion Simple Boiled Rice, cooked, cooled and chilled
    (page 168)
½ teaspoon light soy sauce
½ teaspoon dark soy sauce
Pinch of chilli powder
Pinch of sea salt
Pinch of black pepper
Pinch of white pepper
1 spring onion, trimmed, peeled and finely sliced, to garnish
Handful of fresh coriander leaves, finely chopped, to
    garnish

• Cook the Chicken 65 according to the instructions on page 109. Shred into small pieces using two forks or a pair of kitchen scissors and set aside.

- Heat the oil in a wok or large frying pan set over a high heat. Add the egg, stirring and breaking it up as it cooks. Remove the cooked egg from the pan and set aside.

- Return the pan to the heat. Add the chopped onion and sliced green chilli; stir-fry for 1 minute. Add the cabbage leaves and stir-fry for a further minute.

- Add the cooked and cooled basmati rice to the pan. Stir-fry for 3–4 minutes or until the rice is piping hot. Add the light and dark soy sauces, chilli powder, sea salt, black and white pepper. Add the shredded Chicken 65 and stir-fry over a high heat for a final 1–2 minutes.

- Transfer the Chennai Chicken Fried Rice to a warmed serving dish. Sprinkle with spring onion slices and fresh coriander leaves and serve.

NASI GORENG (INDONESIAN CHICKEN & PRAWN FRIED RICE)

Serves 1

Literally 'fried rice' in Indonesian and Malay, this dish uses just a little chicken and king prawns for a light meal that's slightly sweet and spicy.

½ chicken breast fillet (around 60g weight), finely sliced

1 teaspoon rice wine

¼ teaspoon potato flour or cornflour

Vegetable oil for frying

60g raw king prawns

1 teaspoon Garlic & Ginger Paste (page 228)

1 portion cooked and cooled Simple Boiled Rice for frying (page 168)

1 egg

1 spring onion, trimmed, peeled and finely sliced, to garnish

1 red Thai chilli, deseeded and finely sliced (see also page 33), to garnish

Sauce

1 teaspoon fish sauce

½ teaspoon kecap manis (Indonesian sweet soy sauce, see page 229)

1 teaspoon light soy sauce

½ teaspoon chilli bean sauce
½ teaspoon oyster sauce
1 teaspoon dark brown sugar
1 tablespoon lime juice
Pinch of white pepper

- To make the sauce, add fish sauce, kecap manis, light soy sauce, chilli bean sauce, oyster sauce, dark brown sugar, lime juice and white pepper to a bowl. Mix well and set aside.

- In a separate bowl, place the sliced chicken breast, rice wine and potato flour or cornflour. Mix well and set aside.

- Heat 2 teaspoons vegetable oil over a high heat. Add the chicken pieces and stir-fry for 2–3 minutes. Add the king prawns and Garlic & Ginger Paste. Stir-fry for a further 2 minutes or until the prawns are pink and the chicken cooked through (pierce with a skewer and the juices will run clear). Remove the chicken from the pan and set aside.

- Wipe out the pan with kitchen paper, add 2 more teaspoons oil and reduce the heat to medium. Add the rice and stir-fry for 3–4 minutes or until piping hot. Return the chicken and prawns to the pan and mix well. Add the prepared sauce and mix well, stir-frying for around 1 more minute or until the sauce is reduced.

- Meanwhile, in a separate frying pan, fry the egg in a generous amount of hot oil for 2–3 minutes or until the edges are crispy and the yolk is just cooked.

- Transfer the cooked Nasi Goreng to a warmed serving dish and garnish with sliced spring onion and red chilli. Top with the crispy fried egg and serve.

PAD SEE EW (THAI STIR-FRIED RICE NOODLES)

Serves 4

Encourage your rice noodles to catch just a little at the bottom of the hot pan during cooking – the slightly charred and chewy texture it creates makes this dish all the more appealing.

2 tablespoons kecap manis (Indonesian sweet soy sauce, see page 229)
1 tablespoon oyster sauce
2 teaspoons light soy sauce
1 teaspoon dark soy sauce
2 teaspoons rice wine vinegar
2 teaspoons soft brown sugar
4–6 chicken thigh fillets (around 450g total weight)
1 teaspoon rice wine
1 teaspoon potato flour or cornflour
Pinch of sea salt
Pinch of black pepper
2 x 80g nest medium-thick rice noodles
1 tablespoon vegetable oil
1 small onion, peeled and finely chopped
1 large garlic clove, peeled and crushed
Handful of tenderstem broccoli or sliced green beans (optional)
1 egg
100ml chicken stock

- To a bowl, add the kecap manis, oyster sauce, light and dark soy sauces, rice wine vinegar and brown sugar. Mix well and set aside.

- Trim any excess fat from the chicken thighs and cut into thin pieces. Place in a bowl. Add the rice wine, potato flour or cornflour, sea salt and black pepper. Mix well and set aside.

- Soak the rice noodles according to the package instructions.

- Heat the vegetable oil in a wok or large frying pan set over a high heat. Add the onion, garlic, and broccoli or green beans, if desired. Stir-fry for 2–3 minutes.

- Add the chicken and stir-fry over a high heat for 3–4 minutes or until just cooked through (the juices will run clear when pierced with a skewer). Push the ingredients in the wok or frying pan to one side and crack the egg into the pan. Stir-fry the egg for 1 minute, breaking it up as it cooks and mixing it with the other ingredients in the pan.

- Add the prepared sauce and chicken stock to the pan; mix well. Add the rice noodles, mix well once more and stir-fry for a further 2 minutes or until the sauce is reduced and the noodles are piping hot.

- Arrange the Pad See Ew on a warmed serving plate and serve at once.

DAN DAN NOODLES

Serves 1

These Sichuan-style noodles take their name from the carrying pole (*dan dan*) used by street vendors to transport ingredients and equipment to their point of sale. Salty, spicy and sweet, the noodles are topped with all manner of delicious garnishes, including chilli oil and toasted sesame seeds.

82g dry udon or egg noodles
3–4 pak choi leaves and stalks, sliced
1 teaspoon vegetable oil
100g pork mince
¼ teaspoon Garlic & Ginger Paste (page 228)
50ml water
1–2 spring onions, trimmed, peeled and finely sliced
1 tablespoon toasted sesame seeds
1–2 tablespoons Chilli Oil (page 230)
1 green chilli, deseeded and finely sliced (see also page 33)

Sauce
1½ teaspoons peanut butter
1½ teaspoons chilli bean sauce
1 teaspoon hoisin sauce
1 teaspoon light soy sauce
1 teaspoon dark soy sauce
1 tablespoon rice wine

Pinch of white pepper
50ml water

- To make the sauce, add peanut butter, chilli bean sauce, hoisin sauce, light and dark soy sauces, rice wine, white pepper and water to a bowl. Mix and set aside.

- Place the noodle nests and pak choi in a heatproof bowl, cover with boiling water and leave to stand for 3–4 minutes. Separate the noodles with a fork. Pour the noodles and pak choi through a sieve and drain the water. Rinse briefly with cold water, drain once more and set aside.

- Heat the oil in a wok or large frying pan set over a high heat. Add the pork mince and stir-fry for 2–3 minutes, breaking up the mince as much as possible. Add the Garlic & Ginger Paste and stir-fry for a further minute. Add the water and cook the mince for another 5–6 minutes over a medium-high heat until the liquid has evaporated and the pork is well browned. Allow the mince to catch in the pan a little – the crispy pork pieces are the best bit!

- As the pork cooks, warm the prepared sauce over a medium heat and simmer for 2 minutes until piping hot and slightly thick.

- To serve, arrange the noodles and pak choi in a warmed serving bowl. Top with the cooked pork and prepared sauce. Sprinkle with the spring onions, toasted sesame seeds, Chilli Oil and green chilli. Mix thoroughly and serve.

ANTS CLIMBING A TREE

Serves 1

Here, the noodles are the tree, the spring onions represent the leaves and the pork mince the ants! As you lift the noodles to eat, the pork mince sticks to them and, of course, resembles ants climbing a tree! This is a simple, mild noodle dish, which is surprisingly akin to spaghetti Bolognese.

1 portion dried egg noodles (60–80g)
1 teaspoon light soy sauce
½ teaspoon dark soy sauce
1 teaspoon hoisin sauce
½ teaspoon chilli bean sauce
Pinch of Sichuan pepper
75ml light chicken stock
2 teaspoons vegetable oil
100g pork mince
1 tablespoon rice wine
1 teaspoon potato flour or cornflour mixed with 1 tablespoon water
1 spring onion, trimmed, peeled and finely sliced
Dash of sesame oil
Sriracha sauce (from supermarkets), to serve

- Place the noodles in a heatproof bowl, cover with boiling water and leave to stand for 3–4 minutes. Separate the noodles with a fork. Pour the noodles through a sieve and drain the water. Rinse briefly in cold water, drain once more and set aside.

- To a bowl, add the light and dark soy sauces, hoisin sauce, chilli bean sauce, Sichuan pepper and light chicken stock. Mix well and set aside.

- Heat the oil in a wok or large frying pan set over a high heat. Add the pork mince and stir-fry for 2–3 minutes, breaking up the mince as much as possible. Add the rice wine and stir-fry for a further 30 seconds. Add the prepared sauce and mix well. Reduce the heat to medium and simmer for 1–2 minutes.

- Add the potato flour or cornflour and water mixture, stir well and cook for a further minute. Stir in the softened noodles, spring onion and sesame oil. Mix once more and serve with sriracha sauce on the side.

SINGAPORE STREET NOODLES

Serves 1

This simple chicken dish of curried noodles with added soy sweetness is cooked in minutes. If you wish to cook more than one portion, be sure to cook only one batch at a time. The high heat of the pan is necessary to slightly char the noodles and add a smoky flavour.

1 portion dried egg noodles (60–80g)

1 teaspoon distilled white vinegar

1 tablespoon hoisin sauce

1 tablespoon oyster sauce

2 teaspoons ketchup

½ teaspoon light soy sauce

½ teaspoon dark soy sauce

Pinch of turmeric

1 teaspoon mild madras curry powder

1 teaspoon sriracha sauce (from supermarkets)

1–2 chicken thigh fillets (150g weight)

1 teaspoon rice wine

1 teaspoon toasted sesame oil

¼ teaspoon potato flour or cornflour

1 teaspoon vegetable oil, plus extra for frying

½ red onion, peeled and sliced

Handful of green beans

½ salad tomato, chopped

Juice of ½ lime and fresh coriander leaves, to serve

- Place the noodles in a heatproof bowl, cover with boiling water and leave to stand for 3–4 minutes. Separate the noodles with a fork. Pour the noodles through a sieve and drain the water. Rinse briefly with cold water, drain once more and set aside.

- To another bowl, add distilled white vinegar, hoisin sauce, oyster sauce, ketchup, light and dark soy sauces, turmeric, mild madras curry powder and sriracha sauce. Mix well and set aside.

- Trim any excess fat from the chicken thighs and cut into thin strips. Add the rice wine, toasted sesame oil and potato flour or cornflour. Mix well and set aside.

- Heat 1 teaspoon of vegetable oil in a wok or large frying pan set over a high heat. Add the chicken pieces and stir-fry for 3–4 minutes or until golden and just cooked. Remove the chicken from the pan and set aside.

- Wipe the pan clean with kitchen paper and add a touch more oil. Add the red onion, green beans and chopped tomato; mix well. Return the cooked chicken to the pan, add the noodles and cover with the prepared sauce. Stir-fry for 1–2 minutes or until the sauce is absorbed and the noodles are well coated in sauce.

- Transfer the Singapore Street Noodles to a warmed serving bowl. Sprinkle with lime juice and scatter fresh coriander leaves over the top. Serve.

185

YAKISOBA (JAPANESE GRILLED NOODLES)

Serves 1

Surprisingly made with wheat noodles and not soba (buckwheat) noodles, yakisoba is a meat and/or vegetable noodle dish packed with flavour. Any student who has ever enjoyed the culinary classic 'noodle pot in a roll' will be sure to love 'Yakisoba Pan', a large baguette-style roll filled to the brim with stir-fried ingredients!

1 nest dried egg noodles
1 teaspoon ketchup
1 teaspoon light soy sauce
1 teaspoon dark soy sauce
½ teaspoon sriracha sauce (from supermarkets)
½ teaspoon soft brown sugar
2 tablespoons water
2 skinless, boneless chicken thigh fillets (150g weight)
2 teaspoons vegetable oil
¼ red pepper, deseeded and finely sliced
1 small carrot, peeled, rinsed and cut into matchsticks
1 small onion, peeled and finely sliced
Handful of beansprouts
Dash of sesame oil
Pickled ginger, to serve (optional)

- Place the noodle nest in a heatproof bowl, cover with boiling water and leave to stand for 3–4 minutes. Separate the noodles with a fork. Pour the noodles through a sieve and drain the water. Rinse briefly with cold water, drain once more and set aside.

- To prepare sauce, add ketchup, light and dark soy sauces, sriracha sauce, brown sugar and water to a separate bowl. Mix well and set aside.

- Trim any excess fat from the chicken thighs and cut into thin strips. Heat the oil in a wok or large frying pan set over a high heat. Add the chicken and cook, untouched, for 30 seconds. Stir-fry the chicken for 3–4 minutes or until golden and just cooked through (the juices will run clear when pierced with a skewer). Add the red pepper, carrot, onion and beansprouts. Stir-fry for 2 minutes.

- Add the prepared egg noodles to the pan and mix well, then add the prepared sauce. Stir-fry for 1–2 minutes over a high heat until the sauce is reduced and the noodles are piping hot. Finish with a dash of sesame oil and serve with pickled ginger, if desired.

Yakisoba Pan

Preheat the oven to 200°C/Gas 6. Slice a baguette lengthways, place on a baking tray and fill with stir-fried Yakisoba. Place in the centre of the oven for 2–3 minutes or until the bread is warmed slightly. Remove from the oven, top with the filling and mayonnaise and serve.

WOK-FIRED NOODLES WITH OMELETTE & OYSTER SAUCE

Serves 1

This simple vegetable noodle dish makes an excellent breakfast. Don't be tempted to skip the oyster and sriracha topping after cooking this dish – it provides a sweet and spicy flavour that brings it all together.

1 nest of dried egg noodles
2 teaspoons vegetable oil, plus extra for frying
1 small onion, peeled, halved and sliced
½ green pepper, deseeded and sliced
Handful of beansprouts
1 green chilli pepper, deseeded and sliced (see also page 33)
¼ teaspoon Garlic & Ginger Paste (page 228)
Handful of fresh coriander leaves, finely chopped
1 egg, whisked with 1 teaspoon of water
Pinch of salt
Pinch of black pepper
1 tablespoon each oyster sauce and sriracha sauce (from supermarkets), to serve

Sauce
1 teaspoon light soy sauce
½ teaspoon dark soy sauce

1 teaspoon oyster sauce

¼ teaspoon mild madras curry powder

Pinch of white pepper

2 teaspoons rice wine

½ teaspoon sesame oil

- Place the noodle nest in a heatproof bowl, cover with boiling water and leave to stand for 3–4 minutes. Separate the noodles with a fork. Pour the noodles through a sieve and drain the water. Rinse briefly with cold water, drain once more and set aside.

- To make the sauce, add light and dark soy sauces, oyster sauce, mild madras curry powder, white pepper, rice wine and sesame oil to a bowl. Mix well and set aside.

- Heat the oil in a wok or large frying pan set over a medium-high heat. Add the onion, green pepper, beansprouts and chilli pepper. Stir-fry for 1–2 minutes. Stir in the Garlic & Ginger Paste and cook for a further 30 seconds.

- Add the cooked noodles to the pan and mix well. Add the prepared sauce and mix thoroughly until well combined. Stir-fry for 1–2 minutes or until the sauce is absorbed and the noodles are piping hot. Add the fresh coriander leaves and mix once more. Transfer the noodles to a large warmed serving bowl and set aside.

- Wipe out the wok with kitchen paper, add a touch more oil and heat the pan again over a medium heat. Add the whisked egg and water, tilting the pan in a circular motion to create an omelette. Add the sea salt and black pepper.

- After 2 minutes, increase the heat to high: this will help when turning the omelette. Use a flat spatula to free the omelette from the bottom of the pan and get it moving. Dramatically and skilfully, flip the egg omelette in the pan. Alternatively, you can safely use a fish slice to flip it.

- Cook the omelette on the other side for around 1 minute over high heat, occasionally pressing down with a spatula. Top the prepared wok-fired noodles with the omelette. Add the oyster sauce and sriracha sauce and serve.

7

ON THE SIDE

In many cases, dishes already impressive and tasty are taken to a whole new level by the simple addition of salsa, hot sauce or other condiments and toppings. Salsa verde hot sauce on tacos is perhaps the perfect example of a situation where a good thing is made even better. This is a sharp, spicy hot green sauce made using tomatillos, jalapeño chillies and coriander. If you're a fan of chilli sauce with your kebabs, I guarantee you'll fall in love with the combination.

Many street food vendors pride themselves on offering the spiciest and most flavoursome salsas or house-made cole-slaws. Alongside a selection of savoury side dishes, this chapter contains a variety of recipes for salsas, hot sauces and dips, which can be used to ensure your guests keep coming back for more!

PRETZELS

Serves 2

Soft and chewy, salty pretzels are still made by hand the traditional way by Amish vendors in Philadelphia's famous Reading Terminal market, alongside the classic fresh lemonade (page 262).

80ml milk
½ teaspoon fast-action dried yeast
1 tablespoon soft brown sugar
100g plain flour, plus extra for dusting and rolling out
¼ teaspoon sea salt
1 tablespoon butter, melted, plus extra for brushing
Vegetable oil
1½ teaspoons baking powder
100ml water
Large sea salt flakes and sesame seeds, for topping

- Warm the milk in a saucepan set over a low heat for 1 minute. Add the yeast and brown sugar, mix well and set aside for 2 minutes. Add the flour, sea salt and melted butter and mix well until a dough forms.

- Empty the dough onto a well-floured board. Knead for 3–4 minutes, adding more flour as needed. When the dough is smooth, place in a lightly oiled bowl, cover with a clean damp cloth and set aside for 1 hour.

- Preheat the oven to 220°C/Gas 7. Meanwhile lightly oil a baking tray and dust with a little flour. Divide the dough in half. Take one half of the dough and roll it into a long, thin sausage shape. Holding the ends, spin the dough in circles and it should get thinner and longer. Shape into the traditional pretzel shape, or slice into sticks. Repeat the process with the remaining dough half.

- Warm the baking powder and water together in a saucepan set over a medium heat until the baking powder has dissolved. Carefully dip the pretzel dough into the dissolved baking powder solution, allow the excess to drip off and arrange the pretzels on the prepared baking tray. Top with sea salt flakes and sesame seeds.

- Bake the pretzels in the centre of the oven for 10–12 minutes or until golden brown. Once baked, remove from the oven and brush with a little extra melted butter. Set aside on a wire rack to cool for a few minutes and serve warm or cool completely.

NYC-STYLE CANDIED NUTS

Serves 2

Many a tourist, tired and emotional after a long day's shopping in the Big Apple, has been perked up and picked up by a portion of candied nuts from one of the city's many street vendors.

100g raw nuts (cashews, peanuts and almonds are good)
3 tablespoons soft brown sugar
2 tablespoons white sugar
20ml water
Pinch of cinnamon
Pinch of sea salt

- Preheat the oven to 180°C/Gas 4.

- To a large saucepan or frying pan, add the raw nuts, brown sugar, white sugar and water. Mix well over a medium heat for 3–4 minutes. After this time the sugars will begin to cara-melise. Keep stirring over a medium heat until the sugar mixture has thickened and is easily coating the nuts. Turn off the heat, add a pinch of cinnamon and mix well once more.

- Pour the candied nuts onto a baking tray and spread out in a thin layer. Bake for 3–4 minutes, stirring halfway through to ensure the nuts won't burn. Remove from the oven, season with a pinch of sea salt and set aside to cool slightly. Serve warm or cool completely.

SWEET POPCORN

Serves 4

Making your own popcorn is definitely a good idea for the financial savings alone – it's not just cinemas that hike up the profit margin! Popping corn kernels are very inexpensive to purchase and a little goes a long, long way! If it's your first time popping corn at home, use a very large pot or saucepan and perhaps even start with half of the listed recipe.

4 tablespoons vegetable oil
8 tablespoons popping corn kernels
2 tablespoons soft brown sugar
¼ teaspoon cinnamon
½ teaspoon sea salt

- To a large pot or saucepan, add the vegetable oil. Heat over a medium-high heat until almost smoking. Add the popping corn kernels and stir well. Once it starts to pop, stir in the sugar and cinnamon and immediately cover with a lid.

- Shake the pan constantly over the heat as the corn pops to ensure the popcorn doesn't burn and the sugar and cinnamon are evenly distributed.

- Remove the pan from the heat and leave to stand for 1 minute. Transfer the cooked popcorn to a bowl, season with sea salt and serve.

TORTILLA CHIPS

Serves 1

Once you've made your own fresh tortilla chips you'll struggle to accept shop-bought ever again. That's absolutely fine though as these crispy, fresh chips are super-simple to make and go well with Guacamole (page 204).

4 small soft corn tortillas
Vegetable oil for deep-frying
Sea salt or Mexican Seasoning (page 197), to taste

- Using kitchen scissors cut each corn tortilla in half. Cut each half into thirds to create 6 triangular tortilla chips per corn tortilla.

- Heat the oil for deep-frying to around 180°C/356°F. Fry the tortilla chips in batches for around 2–3 minutes or until golden and crispy. As the chips cook, drain off any excess oil and arrange the tortilla chips on a plate lined with kitchen paper. Season to taste with sea salt or Mexican Seasoning whilst still warm.

MEXICAN SEASONING

Makes around 2 teaspoons of seasoning

This smoky spice mix is great scattered over Tortilla Chips (page 196) or sprinkled over warm, buttery corn on the cob. Mexican oregano (available online from specialist Mexican grocers) has a mild citrussy flavour whereas the Mediterranean variety from your local supermarket is a little more earthy and peppery but will provide a suitable alternative.

¼ teaspoon chipotle chilli flakes
¼ teaspoon mild chilli powder
¼ teaspoon cumin powder
¼ teaspoon smoked paprika
¼ teaspoon Mexican oregano (see page 68)
2 teaspoons sea salt
Pinch of black pepper

- To a bowl, add the chipotle chilli flakes, mild chilli powder, cumin powder, smoked paprika, Mexican oregano, sea salt and black pepper. Mix thoroughly and store in a food-safe container for use in recipe dishes. The spice mix will keep well for up to 1 month stored in a dark place at room temperature.

TACO BOWLS

Makes 4

You can fill these crispy tortilla taco bowls with Tacos de Pollo, Tacos al Pastor, or Tacos Carnitas (pages 74, 69 and 66) or simply add one of the salsas from this chapter and cheese and make Taco Bowl Nachos!

 4 soft corn tortillas, warmed slightly (see method)
 1 tablespoon vegetable oil
 2 x 26 x 18cm (10 x 7in) muffin trays (6-hole)

- Preheat the oven to around 180°C/Gas 4.
- Heat the tortillas briefly in a hot dry frying pan or in the microwave on full power. The idea is just to warm them a little in order to make them more pliable for the next stage.
- Turn the muffin trays upside down. Brush each softened tortilla with a little oil on both sides. Place one tortilla down between 4 of the muffin cups to form a bowl. Repeat with the remaining tortillas.
- Bake the taco bowls in the centre of the oven for around 10–12 minutes or until golden and crunchy. Remove from the oven and arrange on a wire rack to cool completely. Serve with any and all of your favourite taco meats, salsas and sauces. My personal favourite combination is to load the taco bowls first with Carnitas (page 66), then Pico de Gallo (page 205), Salsa Verde (page 200) and Pickled Jalapeños (page 236). Delicious!

NACHOS

Serves 1

Perhaps the ultimate drinking buddy, a bowl of crispy, salty nachos just begs to be washed down with ice-cold Margaritas, Mexican beer (with added lime wedge, of course!) or fresh lemonade (page 262).

1 portion of freshly made Tortilla Chips (page 196)
2–3 tablespoons Pico de Gallo (page 205)
1–2 tablespoons sour cream
1 tablespoon Pickled Jalapeños (page 236)

• Arrange the tortilla chips on a large serving platter. Drop half teaspoons of Pico de Gallo around the chips, followed by sour cream and, finally, pickled jalapeños. Serve immediately.

SALSA VERDE

Makes around 300ml

This spicy and flavoursome hot green sauce is a must when it comes to tacos and nachos. It will freeze well after being boiled and blended, if desired, and can then be fried in a little vegetable oil after defrosting. If fresh tomatillos (Mexican husk tomatoes) prove hard to source, tinned will work very well and can be purchased easily from Mexican grocery stores online.

500g drained weight tinned or fresh tomatillos (around 10–12 medium tomatillos)
2 garlic cloves, peeled
1 medium onion, peeled and chopped
2 green jalapeño chilli peppers, stems removed (see also page 33)
Handful of fresh coriander leaves, plus a little extra for blending
Generous pinch of sea salt
250ml water

- Place the tomatillos, garlic, onion, jalapeños, coriander and sea salt in a large saucepan. Add the water to cover, stir well and bring to the boil. Once boiling, reduce the heat to medium and simmer for 10 minutes. Drain the water, reserving for use later, and set everything aside to cool slightly for 10 minutes.

- Transfer the cooked ingredients to a hand blender with a little extra fresh coriander. Add 50–100ml of the reserved cooking water and blend until smooth. At this stage the salsa is ready to serve and will keep well in the refrigerator for 2–3 days or freeze for up to 1 month.

Variation

For a thicker, spicier salsa, heat 2 teaspoons of vegetable oil in a frying pan and add the prepared salsa (above). Cook over a medium-low heat for 3–4 minutes or until thickened.

ONION & CORIANDER SALSA

Serves 2

Full of flavour, this salsa is perfect with pork taco dishes such as Tacos al Pastor (page 69) or Tacos Carnitas (page 66). Prepare fresh when required and serve at room temperature.

1 red onion, peeled and finely chopped
1 tablespoon lime juice
Handful of fresh coriander leaves, finely chopped

- To a bowl, add the chopped red onion and lime juice. Mix thoroughly and set aside for 5 minutes. Add the fresh coriander leaves and mix well once more. Serve at once.

RED TOMATO SALSA

Serves 2

This fruity red salsa is perfect with Tortilla Chips (page 196) or Nachos (page 199) and works particularly well with Fish Tacos (page 77). Prepare fresh when required and serve at room temperature.

3 salad tomatoes, quartered
½ red onion, peeled and roughly chopped
1–2 green jalapeño chilli peppers, deseeded and roughly chopped (see also page 33)
Handful of fresh coriander leaves
Pinch of sea salt
1–2 tablespoons lime juice

- To the bowl of a blender, add the salad tomatoes, red onion, jalapeño peppers, coriander leaves, sea salt and lime juice. Pulse a few times until a rough salsa sauce is formed. Serve at once.

GUACAMOLE

Serves 2

It's often said that placing avocado stones into your prepared guacamole helps to ensure the mix won't turn brown. In truth, this method is limited in its success and far superior results will be achieved simply by covering the prepared avocado tightly in plastic wrap to prevent oxidisation.

Prepare the guacamole fresh when required and serve at room temperature with Tacos de Pollo (page 74) or Nachos (page 199).

2 ripe avocados
1 salad tomato, deseeded and diced
1 green jalapeño pepper, deseeded and finely chopped
   (see also page 33)
½ red onion, peeled and finely chopped
Handful of fresh coriander leaves, finely chopped
Pinch of sea salt
1–2 tablespoons lime juice

- Use a knife to remove the skin and stones from the avocados and place in a bowl. Mash thoroughly with a fork.

- Add the tomato, jalapeño pepper, red onion, fresh coriander, sea salt and lime juice. Mix well.

PICO DE GALLO

Serves 2

Bright, colourful and flavoursome, this simple salsa combines well with almost anything. An essential topping for tacos and burritos, or simply served as a dip with fresh Tortilla Chips (page 196).

1 large red onion, peeled and finely chopped
Juice of ½ lime
2 salad tomatoes, deseeded and finely chopped
Handful of fresh coriander leaves, finely chopped
1 serrano or jalapeño chilli, deseeded and finely chopped
    (optional) (see also page 33)

• In a bowl, combine the red onion and lime juice. Mix well and leave to stand for 3–4 minutes. Add the chopped tomatoes, coriander, and chilli if desired. Mix well once more and serve at once.

PINK PICKLED ONIONS

Serves 2

These quick pickled onions are tangy and delicious with almost any salad or leftover cooked meats. They make a great addition to tacos too. The onions will keep well in the refrigerator up to 2 days.

1 garlic clove, peeled and halved
¼ teaspoon sea salt
Pinch of coarse black pepper
¼ teaspoon caster sugar
Pinch of dried crushed chilli flakes
Pinch of dried mixed herbs
150ml cider vinegar
1 red onion, peeled and finely sliced
300ml water

- To a large bowl add the garlic, salt, pepper, sugar, chilli flakes, mixed herbs and cider vinegar. Mix well.

- Place the onion slices in a sieve. Boil the water and pour over the onions and through the sieve into a heatproof bowl. Let stand until all of the water drains through the sieve. Place the blanched onions in the prepared bowl of spices and vinegar. Mix thoroughly.

- Cover and set the onions aside in the refrigerator for 1–2 hours to allow the flavours to marinate before serving.

INDIAN SPICED OMELETTE

Serves 1

Omelettes are a quick and easy lunch or dinner but can, at times, feel a little flat or uninspiring. This Indian spiced omelette is packed full of flavour and healthy spices.

¼ teaspoon turmeric
½ teaspoon cumin powder
½ teaspoon coriander powder
2 teaspoons vegetable oil
½ onion, peeled and finely chopped
1 spring onion, trimmed, peeled and finely chopped
½ teaspoon Garlic & Ginger Paste (page 228)
1 green chilli pepper, deseeded and finely sliced (see also page 33)
2 eggs
Pinch of sea salt and black pepper
1 teaspoon lime juice
Handful of fresh coriander leaves, finely chopped, to garnish

- To a bowl, add the turmeric, cumin powder and coriander powder. Mix well and set aside.

- Heat 1 teaspoon of the vegetable oil in a wok or large frying pan set over a medium heat. Add the onion, spring onion,

Garlic & Ginger Paste and green chilli. Sprinkle over the prepared spices. Stir-fry for 2–3 minutes or until soft. Set aside to cool for 5 minutes.

- Whisk the eggs in a bowl and add the cooked spiced vegetables. Mix thoroughly.

- Wipe out the wok with kitchen paper, add the remaining oil and heat the pan again over a medium heat. Add the whisked egg mixture. Tilt the pan in a circular motion to create an omelette. Add a pinch of sea salt and black pepper.

- After 2 minutes, increase the heat to high. This will help when flipping the omelette. Add the lime juice. Use a flat spatula to free the omelette from the sides and base of the pan and get it moving. Dramatically and skilfully, flip the egg omelette in the pan. Alternatively, safely use a fish slice to flip the omelette over.

- Cook the other side of the omelette for around 1 minute over a high heat, occasionally pressing down with a spatula until the omelette is golden and cooked on both sides. Transfer to a warmed serving plate, sprinkle with fresh coriander leaves and serve.

KAI JEOW MOO SAP (THAI PORK OMELETTE)

Serves 1

Seasoned with soy sauce and fried in a liberal amount of oil, Thai omelettes are widely available in Thailand

1 egg
20g (1 heaped tablespoon) pork mince
¼ teaspoon light soy sauce
¼ teaspoon dark soy sauce
100ml vegetable oil
Thai Sticky Rice (page 169), oyster sauce and sriracha sauce (from supermarkets), to serve

- To a bowl, add the egg, pork mince, light and dark soy sauces. Whisk thoroughly until well mixed and frothy.

- Heat the oil in a frying pan to around 180°C/356°F. Whisk the egg mix once more and pour directly into the middle of the pan. The omelette will immediately puff up and begin to sizzle. Cook for around 30–40 seconds on the first side or until golden. Carefully turn using a slotted spoon. Cook for a further 30–40 seconds or until both sides are browned.

- Lift the omelette out of the pan, draining off any excess oil. Arrange on a warmed serving plate on top of Thai Sticky Rice and top with oyster or sriracha sauce as desired.

SWEETCORN CHAAT (INDIAN SPICED SWEETCORN)

Serves 1

Also known as Masala Corn, these colourful corn cups are a perfect sweet salad accompaniment to Chicken Frankie (page 79) or Chicken 65 (page 109). Chaat masala is available in larger supermarkets and Asian stores, or online. It offers a slightly tart flavour alongside spice and pepper to ensure any dish becomes aromatic and inviting.

½ red onion, peeled and finely chopped
1 green chilli pepper, deseeded and finely sliced (see also page 33)
1 salad tomato, deseeded and roughly chopped
Handful of fresh coriander leaves, finely chopped
150g tinned or frozen sweetcorn
1 teaspoon salted butter
½ teaspoon chaat masala
Pinch of chilli powder
Pinch of salt
2 teaspoons lime juice

• To a bowl, add the red onion, green chilli, salad tomato and fresh coriander leaves. Mix well and set aside.

- Fill a large saucepan with water and bring to the boil. Carefully place the sweetcorn in the water, reduce the heat and simmer for 5–6 minutes. Drain the water and return the corn to a low heat. Add the butter. Mix well and simmer for 10–15 seconds or until the butter has melted.

- Tip the buttered corn into serving cups. Top with chaat masala, chilli powder, salt and lime juice. Mix well and serve.

ELOTE (MEXICAN CORN ON THE COB)

Serves 1

Often referred to as 'street corn', these spicy corn skewers are a Mexican street food favourite. They are liberally coated in cotija, a hard cheese from Mexico which adds a deliciously salty flavour.

¼ teaspoon cumin powder
¼ teaspoon chilli powder
Pinch of cayenne pepper
Pinch of smoked paprika
Pinch of dried oregano
2 corn cobs, husks removed
2 tablespoons vegetable oil
2 tablespoons mayonnaise
2 handfuls of cotija or feta cheese
1 tablespoon lime juice
Squeeze of lime and lime wedges, to serve
Handful of fresh coriander leaves, finely chopped, to garnish

- To a bowl add the cumin powder, chilli powder, cayenne pepper, smoked paprika and dried oregano. Mix well and set aside.

- Fill a large saucepan with water and bring to the boil. Carefully place the corn in the water and simmer for 5–6 minutes. Remove the corn from the water and pat dry with kitchen paper.

- Heat a large frying pan or griddle pan over a medium heat. With fingertips, rub the vegetable oil into the corn and place carefully on the hot pan. Cook for 3–4 minutes, turning occasionally, until the corn is charred and golden all round.

- Remove the corn from the pan. Arrange on a warmed serving plate and add mayonnaise and cotija or feta cheese. Rub the prepared spices into the corn until evenly coated. Finish with a squeeze of lime juice, sprinkle with fresh coriander and serve with extra lime wedges on the side.

SOFT CORN TORTILLAS

Makes 6 small tortillas

Masa harina, a traditional flour, can be purchased in Mexican grocery stores and is also widely available online. Making your own tortillas is easy and great fun, however high-quality soft corn tortillas are now widely available online and are also well worth having in the freezer. Frozen soft corn tortillas can be defrosted in minutes or even cooked from frozen. Freeze in stacks of six in freezer bags.

160g masa harina, plus extra for rolling out
100ml warm water
Pinch of sea salt

- To a bowl add the masa harina, warm water and sea salt. Mix well until a dough has formed.

- Empty the dough out onto a floured work surface and knead for 1–2 minutes or until smooth, adding more water if necessary. The dough should be soft and smooth and on the wet side, but not sticky or difficult to work with. Set aside for around 30 minutes.

- Divide the dough into 6 pieces. Roll into round balls and keep covered with a damp cloth as the tortillas are being prepared and cooked.

- Heat a dry, flat frying pan over a medium-high heat. Using a tortilla press lined with food-safe wrap, place one of the dough balls into the press. Push the press down to flatten the tortilla. Alternatively, roll the ball out with a rolling pin. Place the tortilla in the hot frying pan and cook for 15 seconds. Flip the tortilla and cook for a further 30 seconds. Flip once more and cook for a further 15 seconds; at this stage the tortilla should puff up slightly.

- Set the cooked tortilla aside in a basket/warmer or wrap in a clean tea towel. Repeat the process with the remaining dough until all 6 soft corn tortillas are cooked. Use your Soft Corn Tortillas to make Tacos de Pollo (page 74), Tacos al Pastor (page 69), or Tortilla Chips (page 196).

FLOUR TORTILLAS

Makes 10–12 tortillas

Soft and chewy tortillas, deliciously fresh and full of simple ingredients without a preservative in sight!

360g plain flour, plus extra for rolling out
¾ teaspoon sea salt
½ tablespoon baking powder
3 tablespoons vegetable oil
230ml warm water

- To a bowl, add the plain flour, sea salt and baking powder. Mix well. Add the vegetable oil and mix once more.

- Slowly add the water, stirring occasionally, until a dough begins to form. Empty the dough out onto a floured work surface and knead for 3–4 minutes until smooth, adding more flour as necessary.

- Divide the dough into 10–12 pieces. Roll each piece into a ball and cover with a clean, damp cloth. Set aside to rest for 30 minutes.

- Heat a dry, flat frying pan to a medium-high heat. Flatten one dough ball and roll out to a 20–25cm round tortilla. Add the tortilla to the hot pan and cook for 30–40 seconds.

- Flip the tortilla and immediately press down gently 3–4 times across the tortilla using a spatula. Cook for a further 20–30 seconds. Flip the tortilla wrap once more and press down gently again. Cook for a further 20–30 seconds.

- Remove the cooked tortilla from the pan and set aside in a basket or wrapped in a clean dry tea towel. Repeat the process until all of the wraps are cooked.

- The wraps may be served immediately, or allowed to cool completely and stored for future use. They will keep well in the refrigerator for 1–2 days or in the freezer for up to a month. To reheat, wrap the tortillas in foil and bake in a preheated oven at 200°C/Gas 6 for 10 minutes.

COLESLAW

Serves 4

Made fresh, this simple coleslaw takes just minutes to prepare and offers a bright and light contrast to meat dishes such as BBQ Ribs (page 38) or Boneless Buttermilk Fried Chicken (page 111).

2 carrots, trimmed, peeled and grated
½ white cabbage, finely sliced
¼ onion, peeled and finely chopped
3–4 tablespoons good-quality mayonnaise, or to taste
Pinch of sea salt

- To a large bowl, add the grated carrots, sliced white cabbage and onion; mix well. Add the mayonnaise and mix well once more. Cover and set aside in the refrigerator for 20 minutes. Season with salt just before serving.

SRIRACHA COLESLAW

Serves 4

Coleslaw with a kick! This slightly spicy salad mix goes perfectly with Boneless Buttermilk Fried Chicken (page 111).

½ white or red cabbage (or a combination of both), finely sliced
1–2 carrots, trimmed, peeled and grated
½ small onion, peeled and finely chopped
5–6 tablespoons mayonnaise
1–2 tablespoons sriracha sauce (from supermarkets)
Handful of fresh coriander leaves, finely chopped
1 tablespoon fresh lime juice

- To a bowl add the sliced cabbage, grated carrots and chopped onion. Mix well. Add the mayonnaise, sriracha sauce and fresh coriander leaves and mix well once more.

- Cover and set aside in the refrigerator for 20 minutes. Finish with a sprinkling of lime juice just before serving.

SOM TAM MAMUANG (THAI MANGO SALAD)

Serves 2 as a side salad or starter

This fresh, fruity salad is a variation on papaya-based Thai salads and goes perfectly with any leftover cooked meat. Spring onions and grated carrot also work well, should you wish to add some. Serve as a starter with your favourite Thai dishes, such as Pad See Ew (Thai Stir-fried Rice Noodles, page 178) and Pad Kra Pow Gai (Holy Basil Chicken, page 141).

½ red pepper, deseeded and finely sliced
2 ripe mangos
Handful roasted peanuts (see Roasted Nuts, page 151)

Dressing
1 tablespoon peanut oil
1 teaspoon lime juice
1 teaspoon fish sauce
½ teaspoon light soy sauce
½ teaspoon dark soy sauce
1 teaspoon rice wine vinegar
1 teaspoon soft brown sugar
¼ teaspoon Garlic & Ginger Paste (page 228)
½ red Thai chilli, deseeded and finely sliced (optional)
Pinch of sea salt
Pinch of black pepper
Pinch of white pepper

- To make the dressing, add the peanut oil, lime juice, fish sauce, light and dark soy sauces, rice wine vinegar, brown sugar, Garlic & Ginger Paste, Thai chilli (if desired), sea salt, black and white pepper to a bowl. Mix well.

- In a serving bowl, place the finely sliced red pepper. Peel the mango, remove the stone and slice the flesh julienne-style (thin matchsticks). Add to the bowl with the red pepper and mix well. Sprinkle with 2 teaspoons of the prepared dressing, or to taste, and mix well once more before serving.

KIMCHI

Serves 8

Slowly fermented vegetables in a spicy dressing, Kimchi is perhaps Korea's most important food. Served alongside any number of rice or noodle dishes as well as Korean Fried Chicken Burger (page 16), it offers a burst of flavour and is highly addictive.

1 Chinese leaf (also known as napa cabbage)
1 tablespoon sea salt
6–8 red radishes, trimmed and finely sliced or grated
3 carrots, trimmed and finely sliced or grated
3 spring onions, trimmed, peeled and finely sliced
1 teaspoon Garlic & Ginger Paste (page 228)
1 teaspoon fish sauce
2 tablespoons sriracha sauce (from supermarkets)
1 tablespoon caster sugar
3 tablespoons rice wine vinegar

- Slice the Chinese leaf into small strips. Place the cabbage strips in a large bowl, add the sea salt and mix well. Cover with a clean cloth and set aside for around 1 hour. Rinse thoroughly in cold water, drain and pat dry.

- To a separate large bowl, add the radishes, carrots and spring onion slices. Mix well. Add the Garlic & Ginger

Paste, fish sauce, sriracha sauce, caster sugar and rice wine vinegar. Add the Chinese leaf and mix together thoroughly until all the ingredients are evenly coated.

- Pour the Kimchi into food-safe containers and set aside at room temperature for 5–6 hours. The Kimchi can be served that day or stored in the refrigerator for 3–4 days.

BURGER SAUCE

Makes enough sauce for 4 burgers

This classic sauce is perfect on burgers or served as a dip alongside French fries.

4 tablespoons mayonnaise
2 teaspoons yellow (American) mustard
2 teaspoons tomato ketchup
1 tablespoon finely chopped gherkins

- To a small bowl, add mayonnaise, yellow (American) mustard, tomato ketchup and chopped gherkins. Mix together thoroughly, cover and set aside in the refrigerator for at least 1 hour to bring out the flavour before serving.

SWEET & SOUR DIPPING SAUCE

Serves 1

This sauce goes well with Thai Prawn Fritters (page 123) or Taiwanese Fried Chicken (page 107).

3 tablespoons tomato ketchup
½ teaspoon white sugar
1½ teaspoons dark brown sugar
1 tablespoon distilled white vinegar
½ teaspoon light soy sauce
½ teaspoon dark soy sauce
100ml water
1 teaspoon potato flour or cornflour mixed with 1 tablespoon of water

- To a saucepan add the tomato ketchup, white sugar, dark brown sugar, vinegar, light and dark soy sauces and the water. Bring to the boil over a high heat before reducing the heat to low and simmering for 1–2 minutes.

- Add the potato flour or cornflour mix and stir well until the sauce thickens slightly. Simmer for 1 more minute. Allow the sauce to cool completely, cover and store in the refrigerator for up to 1 week.

GARLIC SAUCE

Serves 1

This sauce matches well with any grilled meats or kebabs and makes an ideal dip for fried chicken.

4 tablespoons mayonnaise
1 teaspoon yellow (American) mustard
½ teaspoon garlic powder
½ teaspoon dried parsley
Around 50ml milk

- To a bowl add mayonnaise, yellow (American) mustard, garlic powder, dried parsley and milk. Mix together thoroughly, adding more mayonnaise to thicken or milk to thin, as necessary. Cover and set aside in the refrigerator for 1–2 hours before use.

HOT SAUCE

Makes around 300ml

An essential element of NYC-style Chicken Over Rice (page 170), this piquant sauce also adds a spicy note to tacos or grilled meats.

200ml tomato ketchup
100ml water
1 salad tomato, quartered
1 red pepper, deseeded and roughly chopped
1 small onion, peeled and roughly chopped
½ teaspoon chilli powder
½ teaspoon sea salt
5 tablespoons tinned mixed fruit cocktail
1 teaspoon mint sauce

- To a blender add the tomato ketchup, water, salad tomato, red pepper, onion, chilli powder, sea salt, mixed fruit cocktail and mint sauce. Blend thoroughly, adding a little more water if necessary. Cover and set aside in the refrigerator for 1–2 hours before use.

GARLIC & GINGER PASTE

Makes 1 x 250g jar

If you use garlic and ginger in generous amounts throughout the dishes you cook, it's certainly worth making this paste ahead of time and keeping it in the refrigerator or freezer for future use. A teaspoon added to any stir-fry or curry dish adds instant flavour and avoids the need to peel and chop garlic and ginger on a daily basis.

4 whole bulbs of garlic
Roughly similar amount of peeled fresh ginger
75–100ml vegetable oil

- Separate the garlic cloves from the bulbs and place in a large bowl. Cover the bowl with another bowl and shake vigorously for 1–2 minutes. The garlic cloves should remove themselves of skin.

- To a blender, add the peeled garlic, ginger and vegetable oil. Blend to a smooth paste, adding more oil if necessary. Don't worry about the excessive amount of oil – as the paste sits in the refrigerator the oil will sink to the bottom and can be avoided and used mainly to preserve the paste. Store in a food-safe container in the refrigerator for 1 month or freeze for future use for up to 6 months.

KECAP MANIS (INDONESIAN SWEET SOY SAUCE)

Makes 75ml

Making your own kecap manis is a very simple and cost effective process, allowing you to control the sweetness levels to your own taste, too. It adds a deliciously sweet and savoury flavour to Sriracha Chicken Noodle Soup and Pad See Ew (pages 156 and 178)

4 tablespoons light soy sauce
1 tablespoon dark soy sauce
2 tablespoons dark brown sugar

• To a saucepan add the light and dark soy sauces and dark brown sugar. Mix well over a low heat and simmer for 3–4 minutes or until the sauce is thick and syrupy. Cool to room temperature, pour into a food-safe container and store in the refrigerator for up to 1 month for use in recipe dishes.

CHILLI OIL

Makes 75ml

I've become quite addicted to making this chilli oil and use it in so many different dishes. It takes just a few minutes to make and adds a fantastic depth of flavour and kick – definitely one worth making! Use with Dan Dan Noodles (page 180) or to perk up any stir-fry, rice or noodle dish.

¼ teaspoon Sichuan pepper
1 teaspoon dried crushed chilli flakes
¼ teaspoon paprika
1 teaspoon mild chilli powder
¼ teaspoon Chinese five-spice
75ml vegetable oil

- To a heatproof bowl add Sichuan pepper, dried crushed chilli flakes, paprika, mild chilli powder and Chinese five-spice. Mix well.

- Heat the vegetable oil in a small saucepan to around 120°C/248°F. Carefully pour the hot oil over the prepared spices (the spices will foam a little in the bowl). Mix well; set aside to cool, cover and store in the refrigerator for up to 1 week.

BACON JAM

Makes 200g

Possibly the finest thing you'll ever make, this caramelised bacon jam is like instant bacon. Try a spoonful alongside a fried egg, on top of nachos or simply with fries . . . You'll find new ways to use it every day!

225g smoked bacon slices (around 8 slices), diced
1 red onion, peeled and finely sliced
1 garlic clove, peeled and crushed
3 tablespoons soft brown sugar
2 tablespoons brewed coffee
2 teaspoons balsamic vinegar
1 teaspoon maple syrup
Pinch of black pepper

- Heat a large frying pan over a medium heat. Add the diced bacon and stir-fry for 7–8 minutes or until the bacon is beginning to crisp up around the edges. Remove from the pan and set aside.

- Add the red onion to the pan and fry for 4–5 minutes. Add the crushed garlic and fry for a further minute. Add the cooked bacon, brown sugar, brewed coffee and balsamic vinegar. Reduce the heat and simmer the Bacon Jam for 8–10 minutes, stirring occasionally until sticky and caramelised. Add the maple syrup and black pepper and mix well once more.

- Set the Bacon Jam aside to cool completely. If desired, the jam can be pulsed in a blender to create a more jam-like consistency. Without blending, it will simply be a little chunkier, which may be preferred. Cover and store the cooked and cooled bacon jam in the refrigerator for up to 1 week, or for several months if poured into sterilised jars (see Box below) when just cooked.

Sterilising Jars

To safely sterilise jars, preheat the oven to 140°C/Gas 1. Wash the jars in hot water with a little washing-up liquid, then rinse thoroughly. Arrange the jars on a baking tray and place in the centre of the oven for 5 minutes or until completely dry. Alternatively, wash the jars on the highest setting or steam setting in your dishwasher, allow to cool slightly and use immediately.

CHILLI JAM

Serves 8

Sweet, smoky and just a little spicy, this chilli jam is excellent served alongside your favourite ribs or grilled chicken.

2 red peppers, deseeded and roughly chopped
3 red chilli peppers, deseeded and roughly chopped (see also page 33)
2 garlic cloves, peeled
1 teaspoon grated ginger
¼ of a 400g tin plum tomatoes
100g caster sugar
50ml red wine vinegar

- To a blender, add all the ingredients. When smooth, transfer the mixture to a saucepan and bring to the boil over a high heat. Use a spoon to skim off any impurities which foam and rise to the surface.

- Reduce the heat to low and simmer for 30–40 minutes or until thickened. Once the mixture is sticky, simmer for a further 10–15 minutes, stirring frequently until a jam-like consistency is achieved.

- Pour the jam into a food-safe container and set aside to cool completely. It will keep well in the refrigerator for up to 1 week, or for several months if placed in sterilised jars (see page 232) when just cooked.

GARLIC COCONUT CHUTNEY

Serves 4

This dry chutney is an excellent addition to sandwiches of all kinds and goes particularly well served alongside Disco Fry Egg (page 101).

2 large garlic cloves, peeled and crushed
2 tablespoons desiccated coconut
Pinch of sea salt
½ teaspoon coconut oil
Pinch of chilli powder

- To a bowl add the crushed garlic, desiccated coconut, sea salt, coconut oil and chilli powder. Mix thoroughly. Cover and set aside in the refrigerator until needed. The chutney will keep well for 3–4 days.

CORIANDER CHUTNEY

Serves 4

Deliciously fresh and aromatic, this chutney is an essential part of Vada Pav (page 31) and makes a perfect side with Chicken 65 (page 109) or Chicken Frankie (page 79).

Handful of fresh coriander leaves and stems (around 70g)
1 green chilli, deseeded (see also page 33)
½ red onion, peeled
2 garlic cloves, peeled
½ teaspoon chaat masala (available from larger supermarkets, Asian stores and online)
Pinch of caster sugar
50ml water
1 tablespoon lemon juice

- To a blender, add the fresh coriander leaves and stems, green chilli, red onion, garlic, chaat masala, caster sugar, water and lemon juice. Blend thoroughly.

- Cover and set aside in the refrigerator until needed. The chutney will keep well for 2–3 days.

PICKLED JALAPEÑOS

Makes 250g

Perfect for nachos, tacos and anything else that needs perking up with a little heat, these jalapeños are easy to make and quick to disappear! Delicious served with nachos, tacos, grilled meats or pizza.

120ml distilled white vinegar
120ml water
1 garlic clove, halved
Large pinch of sea salt
1 tablespoon caster sugar
¼ teaspoon dried oregano
7–8 large green jalapeño chilli peppers, deseeded and
    medium sliced (see also page 33)

- To a saucepan, add the white vinegar, water, garlic, sea salt, caster sugar and dried oregano. Bring to the boil. Reduce the heat and add the jalapeños. Bring to the boil once more, reduce the heat to low and simmer for 1 minute.

- Pour the pickled jalapeños into a food-safe container and set aside to cool. They will keep well in the refrigerator for up to 1 week, or for several months if placed directly into sterilised jars (see page 232) just after preparing.

8

DESSERTS & DRINKS

In any cuisine, a good meal is best accompanied by a drink and followed with a sweet treat. After indulging in the best savoury dishes the world of street food has to offer, it's only fair to explore the sweet-toothed side of life. Deep-fried Oreo biscuits, famous along Atlantic City's boardwalk, combine perfectly with Doughnut Bites and Funnel Cake, bringing all the fun of the fair. For a more exotic twist, visit the Philippines with sweet caramelised plantain bananas or head to Korea for Hotteok, sweetened pancakes with nuts and brown sugar. Alternatively, keep things simple with the ultimate street-food treat, Crêpes with Banana & Chocolate.

All of the above and more deserve to be washed down with a delicious cool drink. Healthy smoothies, Fresh Lemonade and Orange Iced Tea are perfect for serving when the weather is hot. When autumn arrives, warm up with a Pumpkin Spice Latte.

Street food is ultimately tasty food and these desserts and drinks don't disappoint, so treat yourself!

HOTTEOK (CHINESE SWEET PANCAKES)

Serves 6

Sweet pancakes, stuffed with brown sugar and nuts, are hugely popular as a street food in Korea, particularly in the winter months.

  4 tablespoons brown sugar
  2 tablespoons roasted peanuts (see Roasted Nuts, page 151)
  ¼ teaspoon cinnamon
  150g plain flour, plus extra for rolling out
  ½ teaspoon sea salt
  1 teaspoon sugar
  1 teaspoon fast-acting dry yeast
  125ml milk
  1 teaspoon vegetable oil, plus 2 tablespoons for cooking

- In a pestle and mortar, place the brown sugar, roasted peanuts and cinnamon. Bash well until the peanuts are roughly crushed. Set aside.

- To a bowl, add the flour, sea salt, sugar and yeast. Mix well. Add the milk and 1 teaspoon vegetable oil and mix well until a dough is formed. Cover with a clean damp cloth and set aside for around 1 hour or until doubled in size.

- Transfer the dough to a well-floured work surface. Knead

for 1–2 minutes, adding more flour as necessary. Divide the dough into 6 pieces, cover as before and set aside for 10 minutes.

- Flatten each piece of dough and add a handful of the sugar and peanut mixture. Wrap the dough around the filling and form into a ball. Repeat until all of the pancakes are stuffed and ready for cooking.

- Heat 2 tablespoons of oil in a large frying pan set over a medium heat. Add 1 pancake to the pan and cook for 1–2 minutes or until golden. Flip the pancake and press down gently using an oiled spatula. Apply only gentle pressure to ensure the filling remains safely inside the pancake.

- Cook the pancake for a further 2–3 minutes or until golden and cooked through. Remove from the pan, wrap in a clean tea towel to keep warm and repeat the process until all of the sweet pancakes are cooked. Serve warm or keep for up to 24 hours and reheat gently in a warm oven (200°C/Gas 6) for 2–3 minutes before serving.

CRÊPES WITH BANANA & CHOCOLATE

Makes 3 good-sized crêpes

You're guaranteed to find a truck selling these crêpes at almost every street food event you can think of!

60g plain flour
1 teaspoon caster sugar
Pinch of sea salt
90ml milk
1 egg
1 teaspoon salted butter
1 large banana
3 tablespoons chocolate and hazelnut spread (Nutella)
Icing sugar, to serve (optional)

- To a blender, add the flour, caster sugar, sea salt, milk and egg. Blend thoroughly for around 30–40 seconds. Set the batter mix aside for 10 minutes.

- Heat a frying pan over a medium heat. When the pan is hot, add a little butter and allow to melt, but not brown. Pour around a third of the crêpe mix into the pan.

- Tilt the pan in a circular motion to create a thin crêpe. Allow the crepe to cook for around 1 minute or until just cooked (if the crêpe isn't cooked just yet, it will prove difficult to turn). When cooked, the crêpe will almost lift itself off the pan at the corners and can be flipped using a spatula.

- After flipping the crêpe, add 1 tablespoon of the chocolate and hazelnut spread and slice a third of the banana on top. Fold the crêpe over the chocolate spread and sliced bananas like a parcel, remove from the pan and repeat with the remaining ingredients to make two more crêpes.

- Arrange the crêpes on a warmed serving plate, dust with sieved icing sugar if desired, and serve warm.

MACAROON BARS

Makes 8

Although stadium food is now hugely popular in sports grounds around the world, these macaroon bars reflect where it all started. Made the traditional way using sweetened mashed potatoes, they were thrown to sweet-toothed fans by a vendor who walked the streets or stadium steps.

100g desiccated coconut
120g floury potatoes (Maris Piper or King Edward)
450g icing sugar
200g milk chocolate, melted

- Preheat the grill to medium and arrange the desiccated coconut on a baking tray. Place the coconut under the grill and toast for 5–6 minutes or until golden. Watch the coconut carefully to ensure it doesn't burn! Remove from under the grill, allow to cool then pile onto a plate. Set aside.

- Boil the potatoes in their skins for 15–20 minutes or until softened when pierced with a knife. Peel and mash in the saucepan. Add the icing sugar and mix well until fully combined. Press the potatoes into a 35 x 25cm/13 x 9in baking tray, score into bars and refrigerate until set. Alternatively, the mix can be frozen slightly instead for easy handling.

- When the bars are set, take each one and dip first in melted chocolate and then into the prepared toasted desiccated coconut. Leave the bars to set once more (refrigerate overnight or place in the freezer for 4 hours) before serving.

CHOCOLATE ORANGE COOKIES

Makes 12

Soft, chewy and packed full of chocolate chips, these are a sweet street treat!

125g salted butter
100g caster sugar
100g dark brown sugar
1 egg
1 teaspoon vanilla extract
1 teaspoon orange extract
175g self-raising flour
½ teaspoon salt
50g cocoa powder
100g milk chocolate chips (30%) cocoa

- To a bowl, add the salted butter, caster sugar and dark brown sugar. Cream the ingredients together until well mixed. Add the egg, vanilla extract and orange extract; mix well. Add the self-raising flour, salt, cocoa powder and milk chocolate chips. Mix thoroughly once more until the cookie dough comes together.

- Preheat the oven to 180°C/Gas 4. Meanwhile drop heaped tablespoons of the cookie dough onto a baking tray, leaving around 6cm/2.5in space between each. If desired, bake just a couple of cookies at a time. The cookie dough will keep well wrapped in plastic wrap in the refrigerator for 2 days or in the freezer for up to 1 month.

- Bake the cookies in the centre of the oven for 7–8 minutes or until just cooked through. They will be very soft when removed from the oven but become slightly firmer as they cool down. Allow the cookies to cool down on the tray for 2–3 minutes before transferring to a wire rack using a palette knife. Serve warm or allow to cool completely. The baked cookies will keep well for 2 days in an airtight container but will become a little firmer and less chewy than when freshly baked.

DEEP-FRIED OREOS

Serves 2

Oreo biscuits are widely available in supermarkets and an American favourite, to the extent of being the No. 1 selling cookie on the market. Visitors to Atlantic City's boardwalk will come across numerous vendors selling these deep-fried delights. Coated in pancake batter and fried briefly, the biscuits become just a little soft and the chocolate just a little melted. This is a recipe you're sure to revisit again and again.

120g self-raising flour
Pinch of salt
30g caster sugar
1 egg
120ml milk, plus extra if needed
Vegetable oil for deep-frying
6 original Oreo biscuits
Icing sugar, to serve

- To a large bowl, add flour, salt and caster sugar; mix well. Add the egg and milk and whisk thoroughly, adding more milk if necessary. The batter should be thick with a fondant-like texture.

- Heat the oil to around 180°C/356°F. Dunk each Oreo biscuit in the batter and place carefully in the hot oil. Fry for around 2 minutes, turning occasionally until golden on all sides.

- Remove the fried Oreos from the pan, drain off any excess oil on kitchen paper and arrange on a serving plate. Dust generously with sifted icing sugar and serve.

CHURROS WITH CHOCOLATE SAUCE

Serves 2

These fried dough snacks are hugely popular in many countries, including Spain, Mexico and Portugal. Often served with a hot chocolate drink, the crispy, chewy texture combines superbly with cinnamon sugar for an addictive sweet treat!

200ml water
1 tablespoon vegetable oil
Pinch of sea salt
1 teaspoon caster sugar
120g plain flour
Pinch of baking powder
Vegetable oil for deep-frying
Cinnamon Sugar (page 252)
2 tablespoons chocolate and hazelnut spread (Nutella)
1 tablespoon double cream
4 tablespoons milk

- To make the batter for the churros, place the water, vegetable oil, sea salt and caster sugar in a saucepan and set over high heat. Bring to the boil and once boiling, remove from the hob to a heatproof surface.

- Slowly add the plain flour and mix well. Add the baking powder and once more mix well. Carefully whisk the mixture until a smooth thick dough or batter forms. Set aside for 10 minutes to cool.

- Transfer the dough-batter mixture to a piping bag fitted with a star-shaped nozzle. Alternatively, shape the churros by hand or simply make churro 'bites' using two teaspoons.

- Heat the oil to around 180°C/356°F. Carefully pipe several strips of batter into the hot oil. Fry the churros for 3–4 minutes or until cooked through and golden on all sides. Remove from the pan and drain off any excess oil on kitchen paper. Tip the Cinnamon Sugar onto a plate and roll the churros in sugar to coat.

- In a small saucepan set over a low heat, combine the chocolate and hazelnut spread, double cream and milk. Mix well and simmer for 2–3 minutes or until the sauce thickens slightly. To serve, arrange the Churros on a serving plate with chocolate sauce on the side.

DOUGHNUT BITES

Serves 4

A carnival and fairground favourite, these bite-sized dough-nuts are great for sharing!

480g plain flour
50g caster sugar
1 tablespoon baking powder
1 teaspoon sea salt
½ teaspoon nutmeg
Pinch of cinnamon
50ml vegetable oil
180ml milk
1 egg
1 teaspoon vanilla extract
Vegetable oil for deep-frying
Cinnamon Sugar (page 252), to serve

Sauce
150g chocolate and hazelnut spread (Nutella)
150ml double cream

- To a saucepan, add the chocolate and hazelnut spread and double cream. Set over a low heat and mix well until the chocolate has melted and combined with the cream. Set aside or pour into a clean, food-safe squeezy bottle for later use.

- To a large bowl, add the plain flour, caster sugar, baking powder, sea salt, nutmeg and cinnamon. Mix well. Add the vegetable oil, milk, egg and vanilla extract and mix well once more. Set aside for 5 minutes.

- Heat the vegetable oil to around 180°C/356°F. Carefully drop generous teaspoon-sized amounts of batter into the oil. Fry the Doughnut Bites in batches of 7–8 at a time for around 2–3 minutes, turning occasionally until golden on all sides.

- Remove the doughnuts from the pan and drain off any excess oil onto kitchen paper. Place the bites a few at a time in a bowl with the Cinnamon Sugar and toss well to coat. Arrange 6 bites per person on warmed serving plates, top generously with chocolate sauce and serve warm.

CINNAMON SUGAR

Makes 1 bowl

This cinnamon sugar is excellent wherever sugar is used, with just a hint of added flavour and comforting spice. It is perfect for dusting Churros (page 248) and Doughnut Bites (page 250). For an instant sweet treat, trying dusting on buttered toast – believe me, it works!

6 tablespoons caster sugar
½ teaspoon cinnamon

- To a bowl, add the caster sugar and cinnamon. Mix well and set aside in a sealed food-safe container in a cool, dry, dark place for use in recipe dishes. It will keep well for up to 1 month.

FUNNEL CAKE

Serves 2

Funnel cake is a popular carnival food across the United States. Although vendors traditionally use a large funnel to drop the cake batter into the hot oil, at home it's more convenient to simply use a pouring jug. Whichever method is used, it's always fun to watch the batter mix web and weave its way into the pan before combining into an odd but beautifully shaped cake.

125g plain flour
½ teaspoon baking powder
Pinch of cinnamon
Pinch of sea salt
150ml milk
1 egg
100ml vegetable oil for frying
Icing sugar and maple syrup, to serve

- To a bowl, add the plain flour, baking powder, cinnamon and sea salt. Mix well. Add the milk and egg and again mix well until a smooth batter is created. Pour the prepared batter into a serving jug with a spout.

- In a deep frying pan, heat the vegetable oil to around 180°C/356°F. Carefully drizzle the cake batter into the oil, circling round and then criss-crossing to resemble a spider's web. It won't seem like it at first, but as the batter sets and cooks, all of the lines you poured into the pan will combine to create one large spiralled cake.

- Fry the funnel cake for around 1–2 minutes or until golden on the bottom. Use a fish slice to turn the cake and fry for a further 1–2 minutes on the other side until golden and cooked through. Remove from the pan and drain off any excess oil on kitchen paper.

- Arrange the funnel cake on a serving plate and dust liberally with sifted icing sugar. Serve with maple syrup on the side.

PEANUT BUTTER & BANANA ICE CREAM

Serves 2

With peanut butter's healthful properties, you can allow your-self a second helping of this utterly delicious, super-simple ice cream! It's a great way to use up old bananas too – just slice and freeze until you have enough to make a batch of ice cream.

2 large bananas
2 tablespoons peanut butter
50ml milk, plus extra as necessary
Dash of vanilla extract
Pinch of sea salt

- Peel and slice the bananas. Transfer to a food-safe container and freeze for at least 3–4 hours or until frozen (bananas will freeze well for up to 1 month).

- Add the frozen banana slices to a blender with the peanut butter, milk and vanilla extract. Blend thoroughly for 1–2 minutes, stopping and mixing manually occasionally, if necessary. If the mixture is too thick, add a little more milk.

- Once the ice cream is blended, pour back into a food-safe container, add the sea salt and mix well. Serve the ice cream immediately or freeze for future use. If frozen again, the mix will become quite solid: simply stand at room temperature for 5 minutes to soften and mix well with a spoon before serving.

255

THAI COCONUT RICE WITH MANGO

Serves 2

Perhaps the ultimate rice pudding, this fragrant, slightly sweet, gorgeously warm rice dish is hugely popular in Thailand and, increasingly, around the world.

100g Thai sticky rice
150ml water, plus extra for soaking the rice
100ml coconut milk
1½ tablespoons soft brown sugar
1 mango, peeled, stone removed and thinly sliced, to
    serve

- To a large bowl add the Thai sticky rice and cover with a generous amount of water. Soak for at least an hour or, ideally, overnight, changing the water 2–3 times.

- Drain the soaked rice and rinse until the water runs clear. Drain again and transfer the rice to a saucepan. Add 150ml water and over a high heat bring to the boil. Once boiling, reduce the heat to low, cover with a lid and simmer for 14 minutes.

- Meanwhile to a bowl, add the coconut milk and brown sugar. Mix well until the sugar dissolves.

- When the rice is cooked, turn off the heat. Cover with the prepared coconut milk mixture (don't stir the rice at this stage), cover again and set aside for 20–30 minutes.

- Spoon the rice into moulds or small bowls, packing tightly. Turn onto a serving plate and serve with mango slices on the side.

BUBBLE TEA

Also known as 'pearl milk' tea or 'boba' tea, Taiwanese bubble tea is now hugely popular at street food festivals and specialist juice bars. Essentially milk tea or fruit-based smoothies with added tapioca balls, almost any of your favourite iced tea or smoothie recipes could easily be turned into Bubble Tea.

• Tapioca balls or pearls are now widely available online in a wide range including multi-coloured and quick-cook offerings. To prepare bubble tea, simply soften the tapioca balls according to the instructions on the product packaging, arrange at the bottom of a tall glass and top with your favourite iced tea or smoothie. Asian grocery stores sell Bubble Tea specific straws, which are larger than traditional straws – perfect for sucking up those tapioca balls!

BLUEBERRY BREAKFAST SMOOTHIE

Serves 1

Super-healthy and full of virtuous ingredients, this smoothie makes for a great start to the day.

50g frozen blueberries
1 tablespoon rolled oats
1 tablespoon flaxseed (linseed)
Handful of fresh spinach leaves
50ml natural yogurt
50ml milk
50ml cold water (or 2–3 large ice cubes)
Pinch of cinnamon (optional)

- To a blender, add the frozen blueberries, rolled oats, flax-seed (linseed), fresh spinach leaves, yogurt, milk, cold water or ice cubes, and cinnamon, if desired. Blend until smooth and serve immediately.

ORANGE ICED TEA

Serves 2

Since writing this recipe I've almost stopped drinking orange juice on its own simply because the lure of turning it into Orange Iced Tea is too strong! Here are all the health benefits and antioxidants of tea, delivered in a thirst-quenching fresh ice-cold drink. Delicious all year round but particularly when the weather is hot.

2 Earl Grey teabags
400ml water
1½ teaspoons caster sugar
Dash of lime juice
300ml chilled fresh orange juice
Plenty of ice cubes, to serve

- Place the teabags in a large heat-safe jug. Boil the water, pour over the teabags, add the sugar and set aside to brew for around 8 minutes. Let the brewed tea cool completely. Add lime juice, cover and refrigerate the mix until chilled.

- When ready to serve, add the fresh orange juice to the brewed tea. Mix well and pour the orange iced tea into a large pitcher or 2 tall glasses filled with ice cubes.

PINEAPPLE & BANANA SMOOTHIE

Serves 1

This is perhaps the simplest and most basic of smoothies to make, delicious in itself or as a base for other ingredients. Add oats, fresh spinach or flaxseeds for an extra-healthy boost.

1 banana, peeled and sliced
¼ fresh pineapple, diced
100ml milk
8 large ice cubes

• To a blender, add the sliced banana, diced pineapple, milk and ice cubes. Blend thoroughly, pour into a tall glass and serve immediately.

FRESH LEMONADE

Serves 2

In Philadelphia's famous Reading Terminal Market, Amish vendors sell this fresh lemonade alongside traditionally made pretzels (see page 192).

100ml fresh lemon juice (around 2 medium-large lemons)
50g caster sugar
500ml water
Ice cubes or crushed ice, to serve

- To a blender, add the fresh lemon juice, caster sugar and water. Blend for 30–40 seconds or until smooth and frothy.

- Cover and refrigerate the lemonade mix until cold and serve over generous amounts of ice cubes or crushed ice.

PUMPKIN SPICE LATTE

Serves 1

A drink which proves street food obsessions aren't simply restricted to food items, this seasonal drink is eagerly looked forward to around Halloween by fans who enjoy the warming, homely feeling provided by the spices.

240ml milk
2 tablespoons pumpkin purée (see Box overleaf)
Dash of vanilla extract
¼ teaspoon spice mix
60ml double-strength brewed coffee (see method)
Sweetened whipped cream, to serve

Spice Mix
1 tablespoon cinnamon
1 teaspoon ground nutmeg
½ teaspoon ginger powder
½ teaspoon allspice
Pinch of ground cloves (optional)

- To make the spice mix, add the cinnamon, nutmeg, ginger, allspice and ground cloves to a bowl. Mix well and set aside.

- To a saucepan, add the milk, pumpkin purée, vanilla extract and ¼ teaspoon of the prepared Spice Mix. Heat over a medium-high heat until piping hot. Whisk constantly until the mix becomes foamy; strain into a serving jug.

- Brew the coffee and pour into a large serving cup. Add the strained foamed milk mix, top with sweetened whipped cream and garnish with a little extra Spice Mix before serving.

Tinned pumpkin purée is widely available, however freshly made is best. Roast a pumpkin (or, alternatively, butternut squash) for 40–50 minutes in a hot oven (200°C/Gas 6). Scoop out the flesh and mash well until smooth.

ULTIMATE HOT CHOCOLATE

Serves 1

The chocolate used in preparing this drink dictates the resulting flavour. For grown-ups, dark chocolate with a high cocoa content will provide nice results, perhaps with a little added sugar. For kids, young and old, use any combination of your favourite chocolate bars!

400ml milk
100ml double cream
60g good-quality chocolate, broken into cubes
Marshmallows and whipped cream, to serve

- To a saucepan, add the milk, double cream and chocolate. Bring to the boil over a low heat, whisking constantly until the mixture is smooth and thick. Pour the hot chocolate into serving cups and top with marshmallows and whipped cream.

INDEX